# THINK LIKE
# A FISH

*The Lure and Lore of America's*

*Legendary Bass Fisherman*

## TOM MANN

WITH **TOM CARTER**

BROADWAY BOOKS / NEW YORK

Broadway Books titles may be purchased for business or promotional use or for special sales. For information, please write to: Special Markets Department, Random House, Inc., 1540 Broadway, New York, NY 10036.

PRINTED IN THE UNITED STATES OF AMERICA

BROADWAY BOOKS and its logo, a letter B bisected on the diagonal, are trademarks of Broadway Books, a division of Random House, Inc.

Visit our website at www.broadwaybooks.com

Library of Congress Cataloging-in-Publication Data

Mann, Tom.
   Think like a fish : the lure and lore of America's legendary bass fisherman / Tom Mann with Tom Carter.—1st ed.
      p. cm.
   1. Mann, Tom.   2. Fishers—United States—Biography.
I. Carter, Tom.   II. Title.

SH415 .M36 A3 2002
799.1'73'092—dc21
   [B]

                                        2001052534

FIRST EDITION

*Book design by Richard Oriolo*

ISBN 0-7679-0995-X

1   3   5   7   9   10   8   6   4   2

*I'm in a boat on Lake Eufaula, one of the largest bodies of freshwater in the southeastern United States, where the surface is as flat as glass and just as reflective. I feel like a trespasser as I subtly invade the tranquillity, my lure marring the watery satin with little ripples.*

*The faint squeak of my reel, about as loud as a baby's inhale, drifts across the otherwise silent setting. Some people forget the real world when they're in a fishing boat. I'm personally so removed from reality that I don't remember what I'd like to forget.*

*Hope springs eternal in the human soul and the mind of bass fishermen, so I intermittently jerk my top-water bait.*

*Each snap, I hope, will be that special action that ignites an explosive strike from a largemouth bass, the most sought after game fish in the world. I have seduced him into feeding thousands of times. But each time carries the thrill of another first time.*

*A largemouth can be as cunning as a snake, as aggressive as a hawk, and is capable of eating small species of each. I've seen bass pick up a minnow and carry him gently for yards, only to drop him so delicately that not one of his teeny scales is disturbed. I've seen bass hit a lead lure so hard that it was dented. I've seen them devour virtually any living thing that will fit into their exaggerated mouth, including birds perched too close to the water's surface.*

*My lure is closer to the boat; my reel is turned for its final revolution. The lure now dangles before me, water softly dripping as it hangs idly in the air.*

*The water separates and the bass explodes skyward, engulfing the suspended bait and thrashing his head back and forth. His tail is a foot above the water. He rips the lure from the line before any part of him is again submerged.*

*It happens in the space of a second. My face is dripping from the gigantic splash. The lure is gone, torn from my rigging by the deep's silent and swimming predator as stealthily as he'd tear one more baby bird from its mother's nest.*

*The mother would only fly away. She, unlike me, cannot make another cast to try to take the bass. She, unlike me, cannot make another and another. . . .*

# PROLOGUE

WE WERE JUST a bunch of good old boys who fished because we loved it when we lined up our boats to await the shot that signaled the nation's first professional bass tournament.

Some uneasy fishermen drove fiberglass rigs, while others rode in noisy aluminum boats that were largely useless, as their underwater sounds scare fish. But the clanging alloy was all they could afford. I remember one contestant even had a wooden rowboat. It almost capsized when the roaring outboards, blasting from the starting line, left their rolling wakes.

The boats floated into each other before the takeoff, and

we laughed at the notion of our being professional anything, except maybe comedians. If we had been baseball players, we'd have been strictly sandlot.

No one could have told us thirty years ago that professional bass fishing would one day be carried on numerous television networks, in this country and overseas, and that BASS, its sanctioning body, would attract significantly more members than the Professional Golfer's Association. And that boats rigged in garages in 1971 would one day be replaced by sleek bass boats, mass-produced in sprawling factories that installed more creature comforts than those adorning many Cadillacs.

Freshwater fishing, by 2001, would be a $108-billion-a-year industry, garnering more profits than any of America's major insurance companies.

When I consented to join the bass circuit, I still didn't understand the idea of going professional with something that I had done all my life, mostly for recreation. I didn't want to turn fishing into a job. I fished the tournament trail for seventeen years until the pressure of competition overshadowed the rewards of angling. While at the top of my game, I walked away.

I didn't make a great living as a professional fisherman because it didn't pay as much in my day as it does now and because I didn't have to. My livelihood came from fishing-related industries. I'd been a Depression-born boy who grew up to start a business with five dollars that eventually generated auxiliary industries and a multimillion-dollar annual cash flow. My Jelly Worm, a plastic lure that attracts bass, and my Humminbird depth finder, an electronic fish locator, became the world's two best-selling products of their kind.

I built an empire off a bird and a worm.

I laugh about it now. But my uncertain future was anything but humorous when I quit a government job to speculate on the idea of making a living from people's pastime—fishing. Some friends and family members wondered why a grown man with children didn't grow up himself and settle for the security of Friday paychecks and fringe benefits that included a term life policy that paid $10,000 upon death.

I think I would have died long ago, at least inside, if I hadn't chased my dream. Because I did, I've often become intoxicated with joy, and must remind myself that I'm not dreaming every time I hook a big one that might just outweigh the twenty-two-pound four-ounce bass that has been the world record since 1932.

That largemouth was taken by a farmer who was fishing with a wooden Creek Chub lure to feed his family. He didn't need my inventions—synthetic baits and radar fish locators.

I feel a kinship with that fisherman from rural Georgia who took the ultimate trophy fish sixty years ago. Fishing for a livelihood is different from fishing to sustain life, and I've done both, as my boyhood was spent trying to outsmart the fish needed for my ten-member family's sustenance. We didn't always eat meat if I didn't catch fish. Sometimes, if I came home without a stringer, we didn't eat at all.

I was under pressure to produce, although I didn't think about that, spellbound while wondering what the mystical fish were thinking about in their dark, silent, and watery world. The more you imagine anything, the more it's likely to become reality. As a youngster, I imagined I was a fish until I learned how to think like one. Most adults wouldn't have the courage to be so uninhibited.

I'm not bragging when I say I consistently catch fish when no one around me is getting a bite. That's just a matter of statistics, as evidenced by my tournament days and my namesake television shows.

When people ask how I bag the big ones, I tell them I think like a big fish. Some think I'm crazy when I claim to get inside a fish's mind, surrounded by scales and gills.

I don't know why my thinking sounds so unreasonable to skeptics. Police, after all, must think like criminals before they can catch them. Hunters must think like the animals they pursue. Athletic teams watch their opponents' game films to learn to think like their competitors.

A fisherman chasing fish will chase them indefinitely, and catch them rarely, until he learns to think like the object of his quest.

The thrill of the chase, not the kill, is the top reward to a true hunter. The ability to outsmart an invisible fish swimming into invisible shelter is the true fulfillment of fishing. Removing the hook pales by comparison.

So join me now on a fishing trip whose lake is the pages of my life. See how I've fished for fish, career success, and personal happiness. At times, the three have been elusive, but I've ultimately caught my unfair limit of all.

Read how I think like a fish, see how you can too, and see what you think about fishing, and yourself, afterward: Seriously.

Dr. Samuel Johnson, an American clergyman, educator,

and philosopher, said that fishing is a sport with a worm at one end of a line and a fool at the other. I understand why Johnson felt that. He *had* to put a worm on his line.

It would be two hundred years before I'd invent my lures.

He'd probably never really fished, just as I, until now, had never written a real chronicle of my life.

I suppose Johnson's intentions were more ambitious than mine, as he, like all true scribes, wanted to write words that make readers think. Not me. I've simply tried to write a few that will enable them to temporarily leave this world for the murky and wet world they can't always see. I just want them to temporarily refrain from thinking about the problems and pressures that go with this thing called life.

No one can think about two things at once. I've never been able to think about my woes when I resorted to thinking like a fish.

Neither will you. Try it. Read on.

—TOM MANN

# CHAPTER ONE

MY FIRST FISHING hook was a bent safety pin.

I was probably six years old, and my mother, Ethel, wouldn't let me have real hooks like my dad, Cletus, and my older brothers had. She was afraid I'd hurt myself. Each member of my fishing family had occasionally let me hold his pole so I could land a fish he had hooked.

Occasionally wasn't enough. I didn't feel that a fish hooked by someone else, then yanked from the water by me, was really my catch.

I wanted to hook my own, even if my hook was a coiled safety pin. I'm sure Mama thought I would never catch anything on the homemade snarl whose lack of sharpness reassured her. She doubted that either a fish, or, more important, I, would feel the pierce of the bent and thin wire.

She was wrong.

I used the makeshift hooks from Mama's sewing kit, worms from the ground, and a "pole" cut from a sapling to entice tiny brim not much larger than minnows along the creek that ran in my parents' 120-acre cotton farm in Chambers County, Alabama. The nearest semblance of a town was Penton, a hamlet so small it isn't shown in the atlas, although it has a blinking stoplight at the crossroads beside the single general store. It had two stores and no light when I was a boy. The place was so small that every resident knew which neighbors' checks were good and whose wife wasn't.

My official place of birth is a rural route outside of Penton. There were no zip codes in 1932. I was delivered in our cabin by a blind doctor. I was one of eight children, and my parents had no money to pay for his help, so they gave the old doctor a cow. Later, when my parents became more prosperous, they paid him twenty-five dollars for each child he delivered. He'd stay at my mama's bedside until her baby was born, no matter how long it took.

I walked to Penton as a barefoot boy on Saturdays, but not for a while after getting my first bent-pin fishing rig. Penton was Mayberry minus electricity, as many of the town houses were illuminated by coal oil. Food was preserved in smokehouses or inside storm cellars. Old men sat on a bench that ran parallel to the only road through town. The old-timers got there as soon as the sun rose, and left as soon as it went down, never leaving their spot unless one got angry about another's move of a checker. The weathered men sported lined faces from too many hours in the sun, gnarled hands that had worked too hard, and invisible body parts that hadn't worked in years.

Their seat was nicknamed the "dead pecker bench." My dad thought that was the funniest thing he ever heard.

As a child, I enjoyed watching fish as much as I enjoyed catching them. I still do today. I was consumed with the fish's survival instincts. I noticed how fish swam in schools and were smart enough to realize that a larger fish couldn't chase all of them. They realized there is safety in numbers. I marveled at how they would glisten in the sunlight penetrating the water, then become almost invisible by simply swimming upright, eliminating the reflection on the sides of their silver bodies. They knew their backs were dark and would not return the natural light to a predator in the water or to the one on the bank—me. I observed how fish congregated behind rocks that stood firm against the current, especially after a rain, when the current was stronger and faster. I surmised that the fish grew weary of fighting the current beneath the water, just as a boater becomes tired of fighting it above. A boater might tie on to the rock to halt the fight; the fish just hid behind it. To this day, I notice that many anglers fish the most open and pretty part of a stream. They should throw their bait immediately behind obstructions, which fish use as a shield so they can rest against the constant flow of water.

Nature has taught fish to think like the vulnerable creatures they are. The fish themselves would teach me, for years to come, how to think like fish.

In war, men are taught to think like their enemy. In sport, contestants should think like their opponents. Fishing is the only sport where the opponent, or prey, is usually invisible. If you can't think like him, you won't outsmart him. If you catch him without thinking, you're not skilled, you're simply lucky. Luck isn't as much fun, or as fulfilling, as strategy-born thinking.

Fishing was never a pastime or hobby for me. It's been an obsession since I first saw a fin. Beginning at age six, I helped my dad and then seven brothers and sisters work in the cotton field on our family farm. Dad bought the place for $2,500. He made payments each month for twenty years before its mortgage was satisfied.

My family sowed cotton seeds by hand on all fours. My dad bought the seed on a handshake loan from a Lafayette, Alabama, banker. Come fall, Dad returned the money with interest. There were no forms or financial statements. Just one honest man doing business with another.

It was a different time, when money was just money and integrity was the real currency.

During the growing season, my family whacked at cotton patch weeds with a hoe and at the snakes that often darted from beneath the plants. In the fall, they picked the cotton bolls from their prickly bushes. I saw their fingers bleed, and I grew to see my own bleed too. After picking it, my family chopped the cotton plants by hand. The stalks were dried and used for food for our few cows or plowed back under the ground as fertilizer.

My job, as the youngest Mann in the field, was to carry water to family members who were actually doing the job. I walked barefoot through the wet rows and felt the mud squish between my toes after a rain. I waded through weeds up to my waist to put two buckets into a stream, then I toted them back to the thirsty folks working the earth. They gave the ground their sweat. It gave them a crop that gave them money for sustenance. The water we drank was warm when taken from the shallow creek and outright hot by the time I toted it to the field in hundred-degree heat.

I mistakenly thought that my daddy, brothers, and sisters didn't know I was secretly fishing while I was supposedly en route to the field with their water. Later, I found out they knew all along.

I couldn't help myself. The stream and its fish were a magnet whose pull I feel to this day. I hid tree branch poles beneath bushes so I could grab a pole wherever I happened to be on the stream. My bait was worms I had earlier picked from the ground. I learned early in life that worms, especially during the dry days of a hot Deep South summer, would rise to the surface, where the ground was dampened by the dishwater thrown from our back porch nightly.

I dug for the worms shortly after daybreak and placed them in a tin can with two holes near the top. I threaded string through the holes and put it around my neck.

I was ready to go fishing.

I caught minnows, and the occasional snake, by folding screen wire and cutting it at the fold. I'd drop a soda cracker into a Mason jar, then shove the screen into the glass and fashion it into a funnel. I'd place the jar and screen into the stream; the minnows would swim in and couldn't find their way out. Minnows were as plentiful as all freshwater fish in this country during the Depression. I could catch a hundred in about a half hour.

Fishermen can catch minnows the same way today. In fact, traps like the one I've described are now mass-produced.

My dad and my uncle Alvin taught me how to do the

Mason jar/screen wire trick. Stripping the screen from our cabin windows was my idea. My mom had a fit. She wasn't at all happy that my fondness for fishing was taking priority over her aversion to the insects that entered our cabin through our screenless windows. I got many spankings for destroying the screens.

I figured the spankings were the price I'd have to pay for fishing. I didn't get as many spankings, however, for screen stripping as I deserved.

That's because we ate what I caught, and we needed every bite. By the time I was seven I could catch and clean enough brim to feed a hungry ten-member family. Mama knew that if I didn't fish, we might have only the vegetables from our garden for dinner. My brothers, uncles, and my dad kept our catches for food. We fished for fun and to stay alive. We hunted wild game for the same reasons.

We drank water from a well, read by the glow of a kerosene lamp, and were housed by logs fitted so loosely, you could see in between them. There was one spot in our cabin where my brothers and I could literally throw a cat through a gap in the wall. There was nothing between us and the elements except a stack of logs. We had no ceiling, and the warmth from our fire rose into the rafters, leaving us cold down below.

I don't remember many snowfalls when I was a boy, but the few I recall left a thin layer of white stuff on our blankets. At times, the wind blew hard enough through the house to extinguish the flames in the lamps.

I've heard folks say that life during the Depression was simple, so much so that families were welcome at the homes of others without notice. That's true, and why wouldn't it be? How could anybody notify anybody when there were no telephones? Folks were welcome at our house, but their arrival was totally unexpected. We saw them approaching through the spaces between the logs.

We had a battery-operated radio, and we gathered around it to listen to the news, hoping to hear that President Roosevelt and his New Deal were improving the nation's economy. On Saturday nights, we celebrated the end of the workweek by listening to the Grand Ole Opry in faraway Nashville, Tennessee.

The rest of the time, we had no input from the world beyond Chambers County. Dad wouldn't let us play the radio, as he wanted to preserve its battery.

Loretta Lynn, in her song about Depression-strapped America, described an upbringing similar to mine: *We were poor/But we had love/That's the one thing that/Daddy made sure of* . . . go the lyrics.

That was certainly true of the Mann family. We had love.

We also had the drudgery that comes from working too hard for too long so our family could earn too little money.

A handful of celebrities got a mountain of bad publicity in the late 1990s because they owned factories where children worked for pennies a day. Those factories are called sweatshops. The United States had no child labor laws during the 1930s and the Mann children were like others in rural America. They worked from daybreak till dark in a sweatshop that was a wide-open field and received no direct income, not even pennies.

The county paid for rabies vaccinations administered to the Manns' livestock as well as to neighboring animals. Human beings were given diphtheria shots.

My buddy and I once ran from a nurse who wanted to give us a painful inoculation. Once out of sight, we slowed our run to a walk along the shoulder of the road. Suddenly, we heard the screeching of tires. The nurse bolted from a car and grabbed each of us, holding us in a hammerlock while she jabbed us with a one-inch needle. She was angry and we felt it, as she pushed that needle all the way to our shoulder bones.

We were safe against rabies. I'm not sure my dad was.

He was once bitten by a cow and had to go to the county for rabies shots. In the 1930s, twenty-one incredibly painful shots were required as an antidote to the fatal disease.

When dad died in 1986, an autopsy revealed twenty-one cancerous tumors, each in the precise spot where he had received a rabies shot.

We didn't know we were poor for a couple of reasons. In a pre-television nation, we could not see how folks outside of Chambers County lived. We thought everyone else in America had a lifestyle like ours. We also thought we were somewhat prosperous because our mother, not a man from the county government, cut our hair. Mom used scissors that resembled sheep shears. They pulled out more hair than they cut. But our cut was unlike the other children's, who had a bowl placed on their heads by a county agent who cut only the hair that protruded. His victims looked like the boy on today's cans of Dutch Boy paints.

Our parents took seriously, very seriously, the necessity of working for a living. My dad once hired a neighbor, Arthur

Butler, to swing an ax from sunup to sundown, chopping wood. Arthur worked for Dad for years. He was paid four dollar a day, plus a noon meal.

Dad retired him when he was seventy-five.

"Why did you retire old Arthur?" I asked Dad.

"Hell, the old shit got to where he wouldn't work," Dad said. "There I was, a-paying him four dollars a day, and he got to where he'd only work from sunrise until five o'clock."

That was the thinking behind the era's work ethic.

Out of necessity, we kids learned how to take a mental and emotional recess from our grueling farm tasks, making our own amusement as effectively as we made our own way.

For me, the happy times almost always centered around fishing.

I remember one of the thousands of school bus rides I took over a bridge that crossed water so clear I could see giant brim from my seat. One time, I got off at our house, got my pole, and ran about five miles back to the bridge, where I popped a real hook in front of the fish. (I had moved past the bent-pin stage.) I let the hook drop into the water as if it were natural bait falling from a tree. Bam! I had won one more round in nature's oldest game—survival of the fittest. That brim and others made up that night's supper.

Brim will not chase bait as far as bass. The trick to catching brim is to get the bait right in front of the fish. At night, this can be done with a tiny surface lure, as brim have a very small mouth. During the day, it can often be done by eyesight, since brim like shallow water. Look carefully for them near the bank in shallow weed-beds. If you're using live bait such as worms, drop it an inch from his nose, and he'll usually strike. A bass, on the other hand, isn't as likely to hit something that still, even if it's right before him. He prefers the hyperactivity of bait that a brim often does not.

When I got a bit older, I stopped carrying water to my family in the field and took my place behind a plow line and a mule.

The first time I put the plow line around my neck I instantly felt the strength of our mule, Old Tom, as he yanked me downward to the ground. I had not learned to avoid struggling against Old Tom's pull or how to keep the plow upright.

I eventually learned to let the plow do the work, instead of working against the plow. That made for work that was less strenuous but still a long way from easy. The work offered sore muscles and little satisfaction. It was a long way from fishing.

I was plowing one day when our old mule was especially slow, and I was in an especially big hurry to go fishing. The mule was actually falling asleep while he was supposed to be working. His frequent stops and stalls were monotonous. Monotony was an integral part of rural life back then, and I did whatever I could to break it.

On this day, I whipped the plow line hard against Old Tom's back. He still didn't move. When I walked from behind the plow, I saw that his eyes were closed. He was asleep again. For me, sleep would be fitful that night if I didn't get my daily dose of fishing.

I yelled and kicked the animal. I was sure I heard him respond—by snoring. I don't think mules really snore. But my eagerness to get out from behind the mule and onto the riverbank was so acute that it made me hear things. I threw rocks and branches at the mule. He jolted for a foot or two, stood still, then fell back to sleep.

The mule grew increasingly stubborn. I still had many rows to plow, and the sun was not that far from setting. My eagerness evolved into anxiety. I knew that if the sun set, I would not get to fish until after another sunrise. Mama wouldn't let me fish after dark, not unless Dad or one of my uncles was with me.

They wouldn't be that night.

I had to motivate the mule or forget about fishing that day. But I was at a loss as to how to make the mule move.

When I saw a couple of moles, I had an idea. It would be mischievous but productive. Just as screen-stripping ultimately made for the catching of minnows, mule-moving would make for a fishing trip where the minnows would translate into bigger fish and full stomachs. That's how I assessed, or rationalized, my plan.

I snatched a mole from the ground, quickly and cautiously so he wouldn't bite me, and inched slowly toward the mule's tail. He snorted, as if he suspected something, but didn't move.

Ever so softly I raised his tail with one hand and hoisted the mole with the other. I began to giggle. I had learned early in my young life that I had to make my own fun.

The mule, meanwhile, had fallen into a deeper sleep.

I guess that's why he didn't buck when I raised his tail, standing it straight up from his back. He also didn't buck when I shoved the mole into that part of the mule where the sun never shines. Once inside the mule, the mole began to scratch, to claw.

You can believe that the mule *finally* began to move. In fact, he moved everything in his path.

He raged up on his hindquarters and let out a yell that made his usual hee-haw sound like a whisper. He lunged forward with such force that he pulled the plow from the ground, then pulled the plow line from the plow.

Totally inside the mule, the mole was now out of sight. Soon, so was the mule. He bucked his rear legs toward the sky, yelled ever louder, and ran through a barbed wire fence designed to restrain a fully grown bull.

*Ping! Ping!* the wires snapped. Two fence poles were pulled right out of the ground before the wires broke. The mule began to run even faster.

Old Tom, earlier asleep on his feet, sprinted for a half mile into the barn. I ran as fast as I could in his dust. I got to the barn just in time to see him standing on his rear legs and beating the wall with his front ones. He knocked down several boards, making a hole big enough for a mule to jump through. Old Tom couldn't jump through the wall. So he stood in his stall and jumped up and down.

Dad came running.

"I ain't never seen a mule jump up and down thataway," Dad yelled, his words lost to Old Tom's braying. "What do you reckon is wrong with that mule?"

"I don't know," I screamed. "He acts like he's got a mole up his ass."

There was a long pause, punctuated only by Old Tom's nonstop noise.

"I ain't never seen a mole climb a mule," Dad yelled. "But he couldn't act no crazier if he *did* have a mole up his ass. You think he does have a mole up his ass?"

I didn't think. I knew. I waited for a few months before I told Dad that there had, in fact, been a mole inside the mule and that I knew how it got there.

A farm family had no possession more valuable than its mule. My trifling with the animal was, in fact, trifling with our livelihood. Dad got angry when I told him what I'd done. When he turned away from me, however, I swear I saw him smile.

Our fun was as limitless as our imaginations, and imaginations were very vivid in a world more innocent than the one Norman Rockwell portrayed years later.

About twenty members of the Mann family were gathered for a picnic. It was one of those affairs where the old men whittled and talked about what was wrong around the world, even though their world stretched only to the county line. The old women sewed and talked about cooking, canning, and children, as if there were no world outside their own.

The children, meanwhile, were often busy contriving the mean mischief that comes from youngsters with too many blisters and too little free time. We had nothing to do. If we hadn't been boys, we wouldn't have had anything to play with.

All the kids wanted to make every free moment count, or at least memorable. If our chicanery produced negative consequences for others, well, why worry about it now when you could apologize for it later? I don't mean to imply that my friends and I were unfeeling. We just suffered from monotony overload and an incredible workload for ones so young. We didn't set out to make anyone else cry, only to make ourselves laugh.

Many of our efforts nonetheless backfired.

One backfire popped when we strapped my younger cousin, Robert, in a chair, bent a limber pine tree to the ground, and situated Robert and his chair in the tree's top.

We then cut the rope holding the tree to the earth. Zing! Robert was hurled skyward by the broken tension from a curled two-story pine. He flew higher than those circus guys who used to be blasted from cannons.

Robert yelled all the way to what we were sure was the clouds, our young eyes widening and our mouths gaping as he seemed to brush heaven. Who would have thought an eight-year-old boy could sail with the birds? I could tell Robert wasn't enjoying his ride. He kept yelling all the way back to the ground, and considerably more when he hit it.

He broke both legs. His folks had no money for a doctor, so his legs were "set" with straight boards taped to them. Robert limps to this day.

I don't know whose idea it was to take a bicycle pump and inflate our dogs. We filled their bellies with air and roared with laughter when they farted. The dogs just roared—period—after running madly around the house with a dozen farm boys in pursuit.

A lot of people might find such "entertainment" repulsive. I understand that. But those people have never been as laughter starved as we were. With no store-bought toys, we had to make our fun from scratch, just the way we made our living. We wouldn't have done the things we did if we'd had alternatives.

Perhaps it was one of our mothers who caught us in our unintended cruelty to animals. I can't recall. I remember, however, that we weren't trying to bring pain to the dogs, just smiles to ourselves. We were eventually told to never again put the bicycle pump's nozzle "there" on a dog.

"That's the last word I have about them dogs," we were informed.

Nothing was said at the time about my older brother, Jack.

We nearly killed him when we put the pump up him.

I knew nothing about the digestive tract or how easily it could rupture, as I held down Jack, screaming because we had pulled down his pants. He kept screaming as another boy put the pump in brother's rump.

The other boy furiously pumped up and down. My brother jerked from side to side. When we let him up, he ran as fast as Old Tom when he was carrying the mole.

The grown-ups heard Brother's pounding feet, his yelling and his farting. My hard-of-hearing grandpa actually asked if it was thundering.

"Funny," he said as loudly as only the hearing-impaired do. "I don't see no clouds no place in the sky."

We said we didn't know. Jack, when he was able to speak, told the adults that we had put a bicycle pump up his bottom and that he now felt bloated.

My mom said nothing. She was too furious for words. She just kept stammering, and trying to express her thoughts.

We took Jack to the doctor, who gave him some medicine.

He gave me a lecture about intestines and how we can't digest food without them and how easily they tear and how people with torn intestines usually bleed to death.

I felt awful. Really awful.

Why wouldn't I? My brother had almost died for eternity—and I was restricted from fishing for a month.

# CHAPTER TWO

WHEN I WAS eight, my dad began taking my brothers, my cousins, and me to a fishing hole about twenty miles away along Jay Bird Creek on Alabama's Lake Martin.

We had no car, so we rode within the back of Uncle Alvin's pickup with his and Dad's brothers-in-law, Harvey, Gordon, and Ray. Uncle Alvin was clearly the leader on these excursions into escape from anything to do with dirt farming.

Everybody had a job on those wonderful outings, from gathering firewood to cleaning fish to cooking supper over an open fire. And everybody had a fare. The men shared the cost of gasoline; the boys provided the minnows and worms they caught during the week before each trip.

Sitting by the campfire, the only light in darkness so dense you couldn't see your hand before your face, was magical. Shadows danced across the face of Uncle Alvin, who spun fish stories in spellbinding words, hypnotic against a backdrop of buzzing insects and bellowing frogs. I can see him now, his facial sweat sparkling in the flickering and glowing firelight.

I'd grow up to become a three-time national bass fishing champion. I'd visit every major city in the country and get the VIP treatment in each. My face would be seen on major TV networks, and my namesake show would draw the highest ratings for an outdoor program in the history of ESPN.

I'd fish with the world's biggest celebrities and two of our nation's presidents, each of whom asked *me* to be in my boat or on my television program.

So what's the happiest time of my life? Seven years of boyhood fishing on a little-known creek whose thick brush hid Uncle Alvin's cozy campfire and all that happened around it. The fire's glow is in my past. Its memory has always illuminated my darkest hours.

I went back to that spot on Jay Bird in June 2001. I make it a point to return at least once a year. I go there in my mind every day.

Jay Bird Creek was a part of my family tradition before I was born. My mom and some of my aunts accompanied Dad and Uncle Alvin on Jay Bird outings back then. One time, a snake crawled under Mom's blanket, and her screams echoed so loudly that birds left their roost hours before daylight, she has told me. Uncle Alvin killed the snake, along with Mom's desire to ever return to Jay Bird.

Uncle Alvin was the first man I ever saw who could pop

off a snake's head by hand. I can see him today, in his bib overalls, work shirt, and brogans, twirling the reptile as if it were a whip, then snapping it. The head went flying into an open sky and my admiration for Uncle Alvin into a lofty orbit.

Uncle Alvin had an immeasurable influence on me. I learned from him, and I tried to be like him. I was obviously imitating when, at age twelve, I decided I'd pick up some cottonmouths. My snakes weren't big enough to hurt anybody. They were, in fact, babies so small that twelve could fit inside a Mason jar. I'm sure they were from the same litter.

I determined that I'd snatch each with my bare hands. I intended to brag to my friends about having handled a dozen poisonous snakes. I would not mention that they were too tiny to have venom.

I recruited my cousin Raymond to help me grab the snakes and, unbeknownst to him, to be sure I ran rather than froze if I saw their mama.

In practically no time, my Mason jar was full of squirming snakes, who continually bumped their heads against the lid, struggling to be free. I was so proud, sure that I had certified my manhood as I stuck the jar in Mama's face.

Mama, who had been peacefully rocking on our creaky front porch, wasn't fascinated by the snakes. She tried to slap away the container and instead knocked off the lid. The snakes shot from the jar and fell into the bowl of butter beans she'd been shelling. Then everything went everywhere.

Some snakes landed on the porch, the beans fell between its cracks, and Mama fearfully danced above, trying to keep her feet off the reptiles. She hoisted her dress like a square dancer and stepped high and fast, as if she were doing the Virginia reel. Raymond clapped in rhythm and pretended to command her steps, like a square-dance caller. Mama wasn't amused.

As the snakes slithered away, Mama ordered Raymond and me to crawl under the house and find the beans.

I was certain we'd instead find one of the snakes. Every time I touched a stick in the darkness, my head shot upright against the bottom of the floor above me. I could feel the bumps rising on my skull.

When I finally dragged myself from under the house, my pockets bulged with beans and my head throbbed from its beating. Mama didn't go back to the porch for a month. I haven't gone under a house to this day.

I had intended to imitate Uncle Alvin and wondered what he'd do if his manly snake hunt was abruptly ended by his mother. I decided to act like him only when I was with him.

I was with him every weekend.

The potholes in the path to Jay Bird were so deep that Uncle Alvin could only let his truck motor idle as it inched the rickety vehicle forward. Going faster would have thrown bouncing boys and their tackle from the truck's bed.

We had an old boat we left tied up at the creek. It was made with scrap lumber that became so sodden, the water acted as a sealant, making the boat so heavy, we nicknamed it "Sixteen Tons." The boat only leaked in the seams between boards, and leak it did, despite our hand-patching each seam with hot tar.

My brother and I would take turns bailing the water out

with a coffee can we kept in the boat. Sometimes the water would get so deep inside the boat that we'd turn it on its side, then go right back to fishing.

One time, a man with a gasoline engine capable of generating electricity happened onto our fishing hole. He told Uncle Alvin he could put the wires from his motor into the water and that an electric current would shock the fish, which would then rise to the surface.

"They'll be on top for about a minute, and you can pick them off the surface as fast as you can pick cotton," he promised.

I think he wanted fifty cents to make a few hundred pounds of fish rise from the creek. Uncle Alvin was suspicious, but he paid the man and positioned Sixteen Tons in the water.

The stranger revved his engine, and, sure enough, fish sped to the top of the water. Uncle Alvin plucked them from the drink while Dad rowed madly. One catfish weighed more than fifty pounds, and the two men struggled to pull the flopping monster into the boat, almost capsizing it. They lifted about one hundred pounds of catfish. The thousands of fish were so thick on the surface that Uncle Alvin threatened to walk on their heads. Why not, I thought? I believed he could walk on water. Almost.

As suddenly as the fish had surfaced, they slowly sank out of sight. They had been up for the entire fifty-cent minute.

I'd never seen anything like that, and I never would again.

Chambers County soon afterward made the electrifying

of fish a crime punishable by jail time. If one of us went to jail, the loss would mean one less worker to feed our ten-member family.

I think the weekends on Jay Bird were also special because I was allowed to eat and drink things we didn't have on our farm. I never thought about who paid for the treats in 1940. Years later, I learned that Uncle Alvin was the Mann boys' benefactor. I wasn't surprised.

He bought double colas, which we were told contained two soft drinks in one. You have no idea what a big deal that was to children unaccustomed to drinking anything that didn't come from a well or a cow.

When camping, we had store-bought loaf bread. It was the first bread I ever saw that came cut into slices. We also had catsup, something else we couldn't afford to buy at home. Such luxuries were unimaginable to us during the Depression. For the Mann boys, every fishing weekend was Christmas minus cold weather. Santa Claus was Uncle Alvin.

Our festive mood always mounted each week on the way to the familiar campsite and peaked as soon as we began to unload our gear. The boys knew that their job was to quickly gather firewood while the men put out trotlines, small ropes with hooks. I watched them bait every hook hanging from the line. I just knew that each was going to snag a catfish as big as the giant the man had raised with his electricity. I couldn't wait to see Dad and Uncle Alvin ease the baited hooks into the water. I had a harder time waiting for them to remove the lines at daybreak.

Sometimes I got to ride in the boat as they ran the trotline. Sometimes they let me hold the line. To this day, I find few things more suspenseful than running a trotline.

I still love what I loved back on Jay Bird, holding the line and feeling its pull by the fish I can't see. How many are there? How big are they? As I floated in our boat along the line during the 1940s, I felt the rope's wetness slide through my hands. Sometimes the line burned my palm. It was the most pleasant pain I ever felt. I'd cautiously lift the line upward, easing hand over hand to the next hook and the next fish, which might be a snapping turtle larger than a skillet or a snake bigger than my arm.

I never knew what I'd get while running the line. I always feared that I'd get something that would get me, such as an alligator.

To this day, it hasn't happened.

After we had loaded the boat with our catch, we eased back to the bank, where orange crates we had placed in the water floated, their tops flush with the stream's surface. We'd simply drop the catfish into the crates so they would stay alive—and captive—indefinitely.

Then it was back to our campsite, where Uncle Alvin invariably made himself more coffee. He'd let it boil so long that it was still percolating when he poured it into a cup. Then he'd actually drink the entire cup of steaming, bubbling coffee in reckless gulps. He was like a magician doing a trick. He'd consume cup after cup of scalding coffee until he had drunk the entire pot in one sitting!

I never knew how he did that. Watching him drink the boiling liquid became ritual, as all the boys and most of the men gathered around the campfire to watch in recurring amazement and confoundment.

After supper, Uncle Alvin would take me upstream in Sixteen Tons to hunt for bullfrogs. At the time, I thought I was selected go because I was his favorite among the Mann boys. Today, I think I was chosen because I was young and dumb enough to agree to paddle upstream against what was often a forceful current.

Uncle Alvin and I shined a flashlight into the frogs' eyes, and they were instantly blinded on the bank. I could paddle the boat or walk right up to them and stick them with a three-pronged gig. We took the frogs back to camp and cleaned them, eating their legs, which, although removed from the bodies, would often jump out of the frying pan. That's the truth.

A fry cook once told me that's the reason frog legs are such a rarity at fried-fish establishments. They taste best when fried in a skillet without a lid. But a few tend to hop around the kitchen floor, and the nation's health departments take a dim view of that.

After Uncle Alvin and I returned with the frogs, he'd show us his mastery of a dying art—storytelling. He'd talk about fish in Jay Bird big enough to grab a little boy's foot and pull him under. My brothers and I looked at each other, shuddering at the thought.

We were sometimes joined by an old moonshiner, Ringo Miller. He always happened upon our campsite right at suppertime.

"Now, Alvin," he said each time, "I didn't come to eat, but since I'm here, I'll have a bunch of those Appaloosa cats."

Then, as if paying for his meal, Ringo began to weave a mood with his own storytelling. His yarns rendered us so silently attentive that the crackling of the fire sounded like fireworks.

Ringo once told a story about a giant fish that pulled his

boat up Jay Bird and then him through the water until he almost drowned. He embellished the yarn with each telling, of course. We heard that outrageous fish story a hundred times and never asked if it was true. We were too dazed by Ringo's voice, which would rise to a boom, then fall to a whisper against the howls of the coyotes and other animals in nature's nighttime orchestra. The overture began daily at sundown.

I have given lectures on survival, a subject of incredible interest in 2000 when the nation was warned about Y2K, the computer glitch that threatened to shut down the world. Although it didn't happen, a lot of folks feared they would not be able to eat, as there would be no workable computers in grocery stores, and that they wouldn't be able to warm themselves, as fossil fuel and electricity are also regulated by computers. I'm glad it didn't happen.

I could have survived if it had.

I have gone hunting and fishing countless times and used the techniques Uncle Alvin taught me to feed and shelter myself. Sometimes I used methods that I taught to myself. I know, however, that my methods spring from the best lesson Uncle Alvin ever taught: People can learn anything they want through trial and error by doing it over and over until they get it right. I guess I'm saying that Uncle Alvin gave me a thirst for knowledge and the patience to pursue it.

I've never read a book about fishing. I've never watched a fishing show on television except to see who sponsors them and to entice sponsors to move to my program.

Do you know how to catch fish without a pole, line, or lure? I do. So did the Indians. So did Uncle Alvin. And he taught me.

Use a rock to scratch a shallow trench, or ditch, that stems off a stream. Line the edge of the ditch with sticks. Place the sticks closer and closer together, shaping them into a horizontal funnel. The ditch will fill with water from the stream. Fish will swim into the ditch. Fish are curious by nature. Add anything new to a stream and fish will enter it. Once outside the ditch, they'll follow the funnel through to its exit. They won't be able to find their way back to the larger stream. Fish will swim into a funnel, not out of it. You can then simply pick them up. That's one way to catch fish when they aren't biting. Merely get them when they're swimming, which is most of the time, unless the weather is freezing.

When I speak to schoolchildren, I ask what they'd do if they awakened one morning and there was no food in the house and none at the grocery store.

"What would you do for nutrition if the world was just you against the elements?" I ask.

They have no idea which berries to eat or the difference between polk salad and poison ivy, which bear similarities. So I show them pictures.

Uncle Alvin taught me how to build a fire without matches. It isn't easy, but it's possible by rubbing two sticks together until their friction makes them smolder. Hold the hot sticks against the flammable fur that is usually on tree bark. Some is too fine to see with a naked eye, but it's nonetheless there. The fur ignites easily if dry, as Uncle Alvin showed me. The fur's flames will ignite the bark or other dry kindling. Put larger sticks on the kindling until you have a fire that's as large as you want.

It's rarely cold enough in Alabama for someone to freeze

to death, but it has happened. Uncle Alvin said that folks up
north or in the plains states are frequently caught in bliz-
zards and are found frozen to death. Today I know he was
telling me the truth, as he always did except when telling
fish stories.

"You might one day travel far from home," he said. "You
ought to know how to stay warm enough not to freeze even
if you don't have no tent or shelter."

I listened attentively.

In deep snow, he said, don't walk until you're exhausted.
You might collapse and freeze in your sleep, he explained.
He said that almost any state with snowfall has evergreen
trees. He said I should find an evergreen whose limbs touch
the top of the snow, which isn't hard since evergreen limbs
grow close to the ground. I should scrape away the snow
down to the bare earth. Then, he said, I should take branches
from another evergreen and make a mattress on the exposed
ground. I should use similar branches to place on the tops of
the lowest branches of the tree.

In other words, I should make an evergreen roof and an
evergreen floor. The hanging branches would be my evergreen siding. I can then ease into my three-sided pocket,
with the tree's trunk behind me. The thick branches on
three sides, and the tree behind me, will hold my body heat.

Uncle Alvin said I wouldn't freeze. I've tried it. It works.
I know outdoorsmen who've gotten lost and have saved their
lives with evergreen shelters.

I also learned how to build "tents" out of long branches.
You can too. Simply stand the branches vertically and let the
tops mesh. Situate the bottom of each branch in a circle about
five or six feet in diameter, creating a structure that resembles

THINK LIKE A FISH

a tepee. If leaves are on the branches, they'll cool or warm the inside of your improvised shelter. If the branches bear no leaves, you can weave vines among them. If you can find no vines, weave weeds or grass, dead or alive, into the standing branches. The more foliage you put into the branches, the more insulation it will offer. Indians did the same thing except they didn't weave plants into the branches; they covered them with animal skins.

Dried or living plants will do well as siding on your protective shelter, as both will block the wind. If the plants are dry, don't start a fire inside. You could burn down your habitat.

Or if you simply want to rest before pressing forward while lost in a snowfall, collect pine straw. Once again, push away the snow down to the bare earth. Lie down and cover yourself with pine straw. I've put myself more than a foot under pine straw, with only my nose protruding. I have stayed warm when the temperature was below twenty degrees. The next morning, I was rested and ready to again try to find my bearings.

You'll never starve to death, no matter how little survival equipment you have, if you catch fish without a line or pole. You can eat them raw. If you want to cook them, put them on a stick of wood or spit. Rotate it over an open fire to roast the fish. You can run the spit into the fish's mouth, through his body, and out the space near his tail. After the fish is roasted, its skin will literally pull from its bones.

Everyone has seen strawberries, blueberries, and blackberries in grocery stores. They grow wild in virtually every state below the Mason-Dixon line in the Midwest and

Southeast. Crab apples grow wild too. Simply pick them from the tree, even if you have to climb it.

My times with Uncle Alvin were as instructional as recreational.

UNCLE ALVIN DIED ten years ago at age ninety.

His body was taken to his house, an old southern tradition, and then to a funeral home before being committed to the earth. The soil he fought all of his life became his ally in death, embracing him forever.

He had taught me how to survive most any obstacle or situation nature could put forward. To this day, I see him in those bib overalls sitting around the campfire and smiling with lips greasy from the catfish. That's how I want to see him forever.

My dad had a responsibility toward his boys, and he fulfilled it. Uncle Alvin had no responsibility toward us, yet he took it upon himself to teach us lessons that would put food into our stomachs in the near term and give us food for thought for as long as we lived.

Remembering Uncle Alvin, and his lessons for survival, are memories I'll treasure forever. Living without them is the only thing I think I couldn't survive.

# CHAPTER THREE

I NEVER CARED much about school. I wish I hadn't felt that way, as I passed up many learning opportunities. But I must be honest and say that I found school boring.

In my youthful attitude, I didn't want to study history; I wanted to make history. I took typing class only so I could mix with the girls.

I eventually got through twelve grades because fishing was an outlet for my classroom boredom. I've told you how I loved fishing as a child. Any love for anything, if it's true love, grows. If it isn't growing, it's dead. My love for fishing has grown with every passing year.

Fishing was my fantasy. My reality was pulling my share

of the load toward helping feed our family. The other Manns grew dependent on my ability to catch fish and to kill wild game. I'm glad they did. I loved to hunt and fish, especially when the result was sustenance for those I loved.

Not long after I entered my teens, I started making my own lures for fun and for money. I had observed the elements of structure fishing, elements I acknowledge to this day. Structure fishing simply means fishing around rocks, brush piles, discarded tires, or anything else in the water in which fish can hide.

I had learned that bait fish hide in structure to escape predator fish. Predatory fish, especially bass, loom around structure, waiting for bait fish to emerge.

My childhood friends wanted to go to lakes and fish in open water, where they thought the big fish swam. Not so. I learned that from studying fish while they were studying schoolwork. Again, I'm a strong advocate of education. I'm simply among that fortunate few whose hobby became his livelihood. Since I got my education mostly on the water, I'll share with you what I learned as a young teenager that has helped me catch fish, and win tournaments, for many years.

A fish is a hunting machine. He goes where the bait fish go, and they don't always go into open water. They more often go where there are underwater hiding places too tiny for their predators to enter.

Eventually, bait fish must eat, so they cautiously ease from their cover, or they dart out rapidly. If they dart, they're especially likely to be eaten by a big bass because bass are impulse strikers.

I learned, by watching bass when I was young, the lessons

of impulse strikes that I teach at seminars to this day. I remember experimenting with a lure that I pulled into open water where I'd seen bass.

I noticed that the more time a bass has to consider striking, the less inclined he is to strike. Ever see a bass follow your lure right up to the bank, then halt his pursuit as you lift the lure from the water? He's trying to determine if the lure is real. He's the most cagey and analytical of all freshwater fish.

My dad told me that, and my own Chambers County experiments bore him out.

Today, I own one of the world's largest freshwater aquariums, where many television infomercials have been filmed. I use that aquarium to study the eating habits of fish. I've learned a lot from it.

I learned just as much as a lad, however, by observing the creek on our farm.

I noticed that if I surprised a bass by flashing a lure before him—that is, by letting him see it suddenly—he'd return an impulse strike. Thinking like a fish, I decided I knew why.

A bass will take time deciding whether to hit a lure in open water because he knows he can. If the lure flashes before him, he knows he has to strike instantly or forget striking at all.

If you can trick a bass into an impulse strike, he'll hit anything that remotely resembles something tasty.

I proved that with chicken feathers, moonshine corks, and broom handles when I was twelve.

I pulled the long tail-feather from every chicken on our

farm. I'd sometimes attach a hook to one and nothing else. I'd throw it beyond a brush pile, then quickly jerk it past the openings in the pile.

I put hooks inside moonshine corks and did the same thing. I decided to get fancy and paint half of a piece of broom handle white, the other half red with white eyes. Then I attached a hook.

I coupled my crude lures with my ever-improving ability to ignite impulse strikes. I got to where I could catch fish on anything with a hook in it that I could flash past the hidden bass.

I even caught them on corncobs bearing hooks. I had to use homemade and improvised bait. I couldn't afford to buy artificial lures, and I didn't know how to make live bait dart into an impulse strike, as I do today.

My reputation as a young angler spread at our country schoolhouse, where everybody knew everything about everybody else who was enrolled.

So I sawed every broom handle, hoe handle, and shovel handle on our farm into pieces, painted them, and inserted hooks. I sold them to the boys at school for ten cents apiece. I got whippings for ruining our tools, just as I earlier had for stripping screen wire off the windows to make minnow traps.

There wasn't much I wouldn't do if I thought it would result in my catching fish or learning more about their behavior.

I first saw a rod and reel on Jay Bird Creek with Uncle Alvin. That's also the first place I ever saw an outboard motor.

As some fishermen passed our camp, I fell silent with envy as the sunlight reflected off their metal reels and shiny factory-made rods, probably of shellacked bamboo.

My dad explained that those little metal gadgets had a crank on them that we couldn't see from our camp on the bank. The crank went around a reel, he said, and that's how the device got its name. It would hold line that would stretch almost as far as a dozen rows of cotton is wide, he said.

I feared he was wrong, but I wanted him to be right.

"And then the fisherman turns them little cranks and the line comes back to him," Dad said. "He don't have to lift his pole like we do with cane poles. Why, he can sit in one spot and throw his line in more places than we could cover by fishing in an hour's time with a straight line dropped from the boat."

I knew I had to own a reel.

I saved the money I made from selling my feather, cork, and tool-handle lures and ordered a rod and reel, a JC Higgins, from the JCPenney catalog. I gave about seven dollars for the rig.

No customized rod and handmade reel with gears has ever made me more proud than my first cheap, flimsy rod and reel. A big fish would have torn the guts out of that chintzy apparatus, and that's exactly what eventually happened.

It's a good thing Dad was around to explain the mechanics of a reel. Uncle Alvin was too busy fuming over the noise of the fishermen's outboard motor.

"Just as well to pack up and go home, boys," he said.

"Them newfangled outboard motors has made so much noise, they've run off every fish in the river."

The "newfangled" motor had to be hand-started with a rope that was wrapped around a cylinder. Sometimes the motor would backfire and the cylinder would retract, almost breaking the arm of the person gripping the rope.

I grew up believing whatever Uncle Alvin said. And usually, he was right. Regarding fish and their permanent fear of motors, he was wrong.

Outboard motors make noise underwater and water is a magnificent conduit of sound. When fish are not moving— that is, when they're resting or inactive from cold water— the sustained roar of an outboard will scare them into movement.

A lot of fishermen will take issue with that.

A lot of them have asked what in the world I'm doing when I drive my outboard today through lily pads or weed beds. The bait fish are hiding in there. The predatory fish are semihidden on the perimeter. The whole thing is a waiting game, especially for the fisherman, who's waiting for one of the fish to move so he can take advantage of a trait they share with people: If one has something, the others in the group want it.

Get one fish to bite and you'll get another who's nearby to bite. That can snowball into a feeding frenzy.

When I drive my boat through plant growth, I let my propeller slice the plants to pieces. It flushes the fish from hiding by destroying their hiding place. The fish are territorial. They want to return to where they were before being evicted.

When they come back to their scattered hiding place, I'm there, silently waiting. Leaves and stalks float all around them. They can't see clearly through or above the water.

When I jerk a lure through the water, the bass see it only briefly as it darts from behind one piece of floating plant to another. Wham! The bass will hit my lure, and he'll hit yours too.

That lesson took years to learn, and it probably would have never been pursued if Uncle Alvin hadn't insisted that outboard motors scare fish away forever. Like most people, I grew old enough to challenge everything I was taught as a child. So much of what Uncle Alvin taught was right that I vividly remember the few things that were wrong.

The fact that Uncle Alvin taught me to teach myself was my best lesson.

He also taught me that if I believed I could do something, I could. The most valuable example of that came when I determined I would live, no matter what.

I was fourteen years old and hunting for squirrel. A half dozen would feed ten of us. Killing that many was easy in the thickets of Alabama before agriculture wiped out a lot of the woods.

I knew that a sure way to get a squirrel was to find a den. Squirrels usually feed in the morning and in the late afternoon. When a squirrel first emerges from his den in the morning, he'll instantly run around the trunk of the tree where the den is bored. He wants to be sure there are no enemies in the tree and nothing dangerous on the ground before he climbs down to eat fallen nuts, fruit, insects, or worms.

I had learned that if I sat in front of a den, where the

squirrel could see me, he might not come out. If I sat behind it, he would burst around the tree and I'd have about one second to shoot him. It made for challenging shooting.

I put my hand into some long grass and heard the noise a split second before I felt the pain. My hand leapt from the patch of grass about the time the timber rattler shot out.

His fangs had gone all the way through my hand. In no time I felt the heat of his venom traveling up my arm.

I had been taught not to panic if ever snakebitten and to think and move calmly. On the other hand, I wanted to be at home, where there was safety and rescue. Should I sprint for the house to get help quickly? If I did, I would accelerate my circulation. Would I then need help or a burial?

I dragged onward, my feet suddenly feeling as heavy as the thick mud that lined the creek on our farm. I felt myself get dizzy, but I stopped only to throw up. I stumbled, but I continued to stumble forward.

I was home in hours that seemed like days.

I put axle grease on my wound and got a lot sicker before I got better. As the sun went down that night, so did my eyelids. I was sure the sun would rise again and sure my eyes would open.

Both did. I was still sick, but thankful that I was alive enough to feel bad.

I believe that one should obey the laws of survival, and I will share more about that in following pages. I also believe that if one believes in longevity, he'll live far beyond his expected life span.

Besides poisonous-snake bites, I've whipped car wrecks, heart attacks, the pursuit of underwater alligators, and direct lightning strikes.

Had I panicked, I would not have believed I was going to make it against odds that said I couldn't. Neither will you, should tragedy befall you. Believe in yourself and believe in miracles even if you don't believe in a higher power.

There is power in unshakable belief. I'm proof—*living* proof.

# CHAPTER FOUR

I RODE A school bus until I graduated from high school. I did all the things that post-Depression boys did to vent their energy while riding the bumpy route, such as occasionally hurling something at the driver, then looking away as he looked into his rearview mirror.

If he looked into his mirror before I looked out the window, I was caught and put off the bus. When this happened, I always determined that I would run to my house and arrive before the bus did.

It was a pride thing.

Riding the bus to and from school provided me with my only semblance of courtship. Farm chores before and after classes made dating difficult. So I always sat beside a girl I liked until the bus arrived at her destination and she got off. Then I moved to the side of another girl.

"You're sitting by me only because Betty got off," the second girl might say.

"I wanted to sit by you the whole time," I might say, "but Betty sat by me, and I didn't want to hurt her feelings by moving next to you."

It was a tired line, but it was the best I could manage. I was better at catching fish than young girls' fancy.

A basically honest boy is a basically terrible liar. I find my yarns for the girls laughable today.

The truth is I didn't want to ride regularly beside any particular girl. Doing so would imply I was engaged to be engaged, after going steady. That left plenty of room for wiggling out of matrimony, but the very hint of commitment, especially for a lifetime, was too much for me at fourteen.

All of that was changed in an instant by a girl who's been with me for fifty years, four children, and countless ups and downs on the rocky road that has been our life together.

The former Ann Brandenburg moved into our county school district in 1946. She, too, rode the bus to school and says she saw me before I noticed her. She also says she knew we were going to marry the instant her eyes met mine.

"That's because he reminded me of my daddy," she says. A boy who reminded a girl of her daddy met the foremost requirement for becoming her spouse in 1940s rural America. Today, young men and women compare their economic and social backgrounds and analyze their mutual acquaintances and interests during a courtship that might last as long as their college years. Then they decide if they're meant for each other.

In my day, a girl looked to see if a boy looked like her daddy before she even talked to him at length.

I didn't notice that Ann had noticed me. I foolishly thought I was pursuing her. She's always had a talent for having an idea and letting me think it originated with me. She's as good at psychology as she is at business, and she's the best businesswoman I've ever met.

I've never lost on a deal when I took her advice. I've never succeeded on a deal when I rejected it.

I was sitting next to her on the school bus soon after looking her squarely in the back of the head. That's all I could see from my perch in the back of the bus, the best vantage point from which to throw an apple core at the driver.

I had to finagle my way into Ann's presence to look at her face. I earlier saw it once, then saw it forever in my mind's eye.

Back in my day, a boy didn't call a girl on the telephone, as there were no phones. He didn't squire her at school, as the boys played on one part of the playground, the girls on the other. He didn't sit by her in class, as seating was assigned.

He instead went to her house, where he courted the entire family.

I remember when my sisters brought home boyfriends. My brothers and I never liked them because we thought they had the same improper incentives toward girls that we had. I tried to take my share of liberties with every girl I met, except Ann.

My brothers and I ran off almost every boy that our

sisters brought home. They got mad at us for that, but we thought they were naive as to what the boys really wanted from them. We thought their boyfriends were geeks.

Most of the boys got the hint when four of the Mann boys said something like "You know, if we were at your house right now, we'd probably be leaving—and we probably would never come back."

The boy would stutter and depart. My sisters would yell and cry. But they knew we loved them.

I remember one guy who just wouldn't take the hint. I had put molasses on his car, and it must have taken him days to get it clean. Why would a boy return to a house where he had experienced such vandalism? Return he did.

He and my sister, who asked not to be identified, were sitting on a sofa in the front room, which would be called the living room or parlor today. My brothers and I kept walking through the room so the poor guy couldn't make eye contact without our noticing.

When he tried to hold my sister's hand, I asked if there wasn't enough room on his end of the couch for both of his hands.

"Huh?" he said, blinking.

I dropped little hints like that.

The guy continued to hang around. My sister asked to have a word with me and whispered so angrily that she could clearly be heard in the living room inside a house a mile away. Almost.

Then it was back to her boyfriend and the making of moon eyes. I'd had enough.

I sneaked behind their perch on the couch, which sat in

the middle of the room. I began to clean one of the minks I had caught. A mink has a sack filled with musk. If ruptured, an odor emanates that is stronger than a skunk's.

I did not accidentally rupture the mink's sack. I intentionally sliced and sliced it again. The offensive ooze dripped off my hands and filled the parlor. A sanitary landfill never smelled as bad.

The boy covered his mouth and I figured my plan was working. How could he kiss my sister with his fingers across his lips?

"I'd better be going," he said suddenly, and bolted for the door.

I extended my bloody and smelly hand.

"Good to see ya, pal," I said.

He didn't shake my hand. His body, however, seemed to be quivering.

Neither she nor I ever saw that guy again.

I sat many nights in Ann's parlor or living room, where I nervously let my eyes scan the ceiling and floor. Whenever I glanced at Ann's parents, they were always looking squarely at—and through—me. I hated that, so much so that I could feel myself sweating. I'd sometimes wipe my brow with my fingers when I thought no one was looking.

Her parents always caught me.

"Are you hot, Tom?" one would ask.

"A little," I initially responded. "It's always so hot this time of year."

It was December.

Ann was always the last to enter the room, after her parents had analyzed me, her brothers and sisters had pestered me, and her dog had snapped at me. She didn't merely enter the room. She filled it.

She was walking radiance, flesh and blood poetry in motion. She would have floated had her feet not touched the floor.

I made mindless talk about our cotton crop and fishing and other things that her daddy thought were only the utterances of a boy. Then I squirmed some more.

The ritual of my looking at them look at me went on for weeks before Ann and I were allowed to take a giant step forward in our courtship.

I asked her if I could ask her in front of her parents to sit with me in the porch swing. She said that I could and so I did.

We moved to the swing, just Ann and me—and her mother. If I had put my arm around Ann, it would have first gone around her mom.

She sat between us.

Ann's mother took up plenty of room, her laced shoes planted squarely on the floor, her knees apart under her apron. I would have had to tie a back scratcher to my wrist in order to extend my reach to Ann behind her mom's back.

"Ain't it a pretty evening?" her mom always said. "I just love it when it's this dark."

Move into the house, Mom, I thought. Then I can try to make some fireworks that will light up the night.

My notion of fireworks was holding Ann's hand for a few weeks' worth of visits, after which I'd get the nerve to steal a kiss.

Al Capone was the nation's mastermind criminal. But not even he would have been able to steal a kiss or anything else on that front porch under Mama's glare.

THE REMAINDER OF my teenage years was spent dreading school and anticipating Ann. Once I began sitting with her on the school bus, I never rode with anyone else. It was just the two of us and forty-five jeering kids, some of whom scratched "Tom Loves Ann" on the back of the bus seats. One such inscription had a sketched halo above Ann's name. The other had a cyclops above mine.

Because I loved the outdoors, because I needed money and because I wanted to impress Ann and her people with what a future I had as a businessman, I began to trap and sell animal pelts. I sent them to Sears, Roebuck and Co. in Chicago, Illinois. I was paid five dollars for each beaver pelt and more for a mink, depending on its size.

Uncle Alvin and Dad had told me how the Indians made traps by digging a hole and covering it with brittle brush. Whenever a small animal walked across the hole, it would fall through.

I taught myself about a mink's dislike of water. I found a creek that I knew a mink wouldn't cross. So I set a trap under a bridge where no water flowed. The mink wouldn't swim as a beaver would. He'd instead walk on a little section of dry land, and unknowingly walk across my trap. Clang. I'd have him and whatever money the market would bear.

I learned to build and run traps as efficiently as any Cherokee brave ever did. I even took foxes, my first captives.

Foxes were a real problem during the Depression and the years afterward. Driven by hunger, they would dart into a farmer's chicken yard in broad daylight and steal the birds the farmer depended on for eggs and meat. They would also ease their way into the henhouse at night. The farmer and his family would be awakened by the panicked squawking of the chickens. By the time the farmer got to the henhouse with a shotgun, the fox and one of the chickens were usually gone.

To combat this, and an outbreak of rabies in foxes, county governments throughout Alabama imposed bounties on foxtails. I could get two dollars for each tail I took to the courthouse.

I determined I'd grow rich by capturing foxes that ran wild on our farm and for miles beyond.

I vividly remember looking into a trap and seeing the first fox I ever caught. Foxes had always been so fast and ferocious, I had thought. Why did this little guy have such pleading eyes? If he could have spoken, I was sure he would have begged for his life—the life I couldn't bring myself to take.

I had broken the ice to wade through freezing streams to catch beaver and mink, many of which were dead by the time I found them entrapped. My first fox was alive and full of energy and the yearning to be free.

I couldn't take his life. Then I remembered that no one had asked me to. The bounty was for foxtails.

I used a hatchet to chop off the tail, being sure not to chop too close to his body. He ran through the woods, and I ran to the courthouse to collect my bounty.

Not long afterward, I began to hear the old-timers talk

about the "dangest thang I ever seen, a bob-tailed fox with nary a tail."

Another would chime in that he, too, had seen the same red fox, and the small animal grew larger and larger in legend around Penton, Alabama. Each time his reputation grew loftier, I smiled warmly inside. I've never told anyone that I took the taxpayers' money for a fox I set free. Until now.

I wondered if I had done the right thing only once. I was seventeen when a fox, normally a frightened animal, shot from out of the woods into an open field and attacked me. He bit me three times on the lower leg, which was protected by a thick rubber boot. I kicked the fox off me, but he returned each time with a vengeance. He was aggressive, biting and clawing and screaming like a wild dog. I kicked that hysterical animal so hard that he shot backward through the air for perhaps six feet. As soon as he rose to all fours, he charged again. The fox, which might have weighed twenty pounds, was trying to eat me alive. His teeth had perforated my boots, and my pant legs were torn to shreds.

A neighbor shot him dead while he clung to my pants.

I knew all about rabies from a painfully vivid memory.

I went to a doctor, who examined my scratches and said my skin was not broken.

Then he noticed my hands.

I had scratched them heavily while parting briars. My palms and the backs of my hands were a map of thin lines of torn skin.

"If that fox was mad," the doctor began.

"Doc, I *know* he was mad," I said. "A fox don't act that way, and I seen him frothing at the mouth."

The doctor was thoughtful. I broke the silence.

"I'm mad too," I said. "Look here at how he tore my britches to pieces."

"It's no laughing matter," the doctor snapped. "There is nothing to kid about here."

I had been around authority enough in my life to know not to question it. The doctor was not simply serious, he was solemn.

"If any of that fox's saliva got into one of these open wounds on your hand, and if he was mad, as you say he was, then you'll likely contract rabies," the doctor said.

I knew the answer to the question I was about to ask. I just didn't want to hear it. Perhaps I was hoping the doctor had come across a miracle cure since my dad had taken those rabies shots I mentioned earlier.

"So, what if I get them rabies?" I asked.

"You'll die," the doctor said.

His words were followed by the loudest silence I ever heard.

I said earlier that I've somehow thought that I would live forever. I obviously don't mean that literally. I just mean that I not only don't fear death, I don't even think about it, no matter how dire my circumstances. Besides, I believe in an afterlife and a previous life. My body will one day be laid in the ground. My spirit, the essence of life, never will.

It has been on this earth before, it is here now, and it will be here again.

I don't know if I had thought all of that out by age seventeen, but even then I had no notions of dying.

That's why I declined the rabies shots.

"We can give you shots, twenty-one of them," the doctor said. "They'll be the most painful things you ever went through. There is a fifty-fifty chance they'll totally prevent your contracting rabies. You might take them and live, or you might take them and die anyhow."

I didn't like the odds. And I didn't like the memory of the pain and sickness Dad had gone through with rabies shots given after he was bitten by a mad cow.

"If I don't take them shots, will there still be a chance that I won't catch no rabies?" I asked the doctor.

"Of course," he said. "But the chances that you will contract rabies outweigh the chances that you won't."

He described the long and painful death that besets a person with incurable rabies.

I'd never seen anything like he described. It was worse than what I saw my dad undergo. Even though the shots had saved my dad's life, there were times he was convinced he was going to die, given his adverse reaction to the serum.

I'm sure that rabies shots were far more underdeveloped in that day and time than they are today.

Again I told the doctor to put away his syringe.

He told me I'd know whether I had rabies in twenty-one days. I told him I'd see him in three weeks.

There was a bonding among families in pre-television America like people don't often see today. My brothers and sisters and I fought, played horrible tricks on each other, and did cute and ingenious things to get one to look away while another snatched the last biscuit off his dinner plate.

There isn't much we wouldn't do to each other, yet we wouldn't let an outsider do anything to one of us. If someone attacked one, he attacked the entire family.

THINK LIKE A FISH

This time the attacker was a pending, and possibly fatal, disease.

I noticed that my brothers would thereafter chop an extra row or two of cotton in part of the field I was supposed to cut. I noticed that my sisters, who fiercely competed with me for Mom's homemade apple pie, suddenly decided they didn't want any dessert. Whenever anyone in the family spoke to me, it was in soft tones.

Neither my dad nor any of his children found it easy to say "I love you." But somebody put a note with those words on the calendar where I was marking off the twenty-one days.

I didn't talk a lot myself during that time. Occasionally, a kid at school might say something smart about my thoughtful silence.

It was usually something original, like "Cat got your tongue?"

He usually didn't talk long. One or two of my brothers, who also said little or nothing, proceeded to quietly knock the fire out of him.

"What did I do?" the kid might ask, his nose bleeding on the ground. His question was met with more silence.

Every member of the Mann family knew I was fighting for my life. Each night I fought for the sleep that wouldn't come. But my supper always came up, as I sweated and violently shook with what some were already whispering was rabies.

People living in America's cities didn't know that much about rabies in that day and time. Those of us in the backwoods knew less.

I wondered if I should have taken the shots. I wondered

why I was wondering now that it was too late to do anything except wait.

I lived a year during my twenty-one-day vigil. On the twenty-second, I wasn't sick. The sickness, whether rabies or whatever, had come on gradually and had departed instantly. I rose with the sun to pillow fights with my energized siblings.

I never understood why my sisters hit me so forcefully while softly crying. At seventeen, I decided Ann was not the only girl I didn't understand.

## CHAPTER FIVE

ANN AND I went to town to see movies on Saturdays. Her parents didn't hesitate to let us be alone in daylight—or even in a darkened theater, as long as it was filled with a hundred rowdy youngsters. Her folks figured the boys, always eager to play pranks on a buddy with a date, would be adequate chaperons.

I always had one dollar to take to the movies. It would buy two tickets, a sack of popcorn, and two soft drinks. I squirmed in my seat, fearing Ann would ask for a second drink, which I couldn't afford. She never asked.

Years later, I told her that her satisfaction with one drink was good, because I couldn't have paid for a second.

"I know," she said. "That's why I never asked."

I never fooled Ann, even *before* we were married.

I became old enough to drive our family vehicle, an old pickup truck that whined like a motorized banshee. Ann sat on her front porch and listened for my arrival on Wednesdays, Saturdays, and Sundays. Those were the days a two-member committee composed of her daddy and mama decided that I could call on Ann.

Our old family truck was so loud that Ann could hear me before she saw me. So could her neighbors, who instantly yelled for their children to get out of the road. The rickety pickup had loose tie-rods, which made steering difficult. I aimed for the middle of two-lane roads but occasionally veered onto the shoulders.

I craved that rite of passage that is a part of male youth: the purchase of my own car. Ann wanted me to have it too. My first car would be a big deal for both of us, as it would provide a chance for us to be alone. There was no room in a Ford coupe for Ann's mom to hang a porch swing and sit between us.

Ann helped me put aside part of my money from trapping, embarking on what would become her lifelong practice of managing my cash flow.

I finally saved enough to buy my first car. No one would have mistaken it for a limousine. I steered with one hand while using the other to hold the driver's door shut.

Ann and I had grown into our first car, but there were growing pains.

I had taken Ann home one evening and shaken her hand good night under the watchful, approving gaze of her family. I was on the way back to my house when a possum crossed the road in front of me. I was still the main meat provider for our clan, and possum was one of the many meats we ate.

I stopped the car, caught the possum by hand, and resumed my drive with what I was sure would be an easy dinner. I went to sleep and so did the possum—only he went to sleep right inside my car, right where I forgot him.

I also forgot to look for him the next day, when he would have been easy to find because he couldn't run. He had died. Three days after his death, in the sweltering Alabama heat, my car reeked, although I didn't know why.

Ann was polite. She said she thought she detected an unpleasant odor. I was realistic. I said I hoped the car's paint didn't peel.

Ann was a meticulous dresser, as she is today. She didn't like to travel with the windows down, as the breeze messed her hair. There wasn't exactly a breeze through my old car. It was more like a tornado. I drove with all four windows wide open to air out what had become a graveyard on wheels. The decaying animal was permanently playing possum.

Talk about romantic.

"What in the world is that smell?" Ann finally asked as she choked on the stench.

"Must be the paint burning off the motor," I said.

"There isn't enough paint on the motor or anywhere else on this car to make a smell that bad," she said.

I wound up taking the seats out of the car and finding the remains. What a beginning for our highly anticipated motorized courtship.

I'VE INTENTIONALLY PAINTED a picture of the simple life that was mine until I became a young adult. We were simple people with simple ways. Sometimes, that was simply hard to live with.

When I was in high school, teachers could paddle students for something as insignificant as talking in class. Can you imagine what would happen if a teacher did that today?

In a small community where the first language was word of mouth, parents usually knew a child had been whipped before he got home from school. Their reaction was to whip him or her again. America's fighting forces were battling the Japanese and Germans overseas. The fighting spirit was alive in rural America, except the targets of assault—children and teenagers—didn't dare strike back. Today's parents are urged to get to know their children. My generation's parents were urged to discipline children—with force.

If you broke rules, no matter how ridiculous, your punishment was swift and stern. And simple.

Justice was just as simple when it was a reflex response in the form of deadly violence. I saw that firsthand with one of Dad's paid hands, T. B. Bailey, a black man who hired out to area farmers to help chop cotton and do other farmwork.

Bailey worked from before sunrise until after sundown for pennies. His recreation, for lack of a better word, was a nickel's worth of moonshine whiskey drunk while playing penny-ante poker. A field-worker could get falling-down drunk and win or lose as much as a dime, all for less than twenty cents per game. A game might afford hours of "entertainment."

The farmworkers looked forward to the mental escape all week.

Bailey was winning hand after hand in a poker game held in a ramshackle shack. No landowners or their kids were admitted—just the poor black field hands. Rumor had it that the workers would throw in a nickel each for a woman who would "visit" with all of them. If so, that was something else that happened behind closed doors in a closed society.

Bailey parlayed his streak of luck into winnings of five cents. He cashed in his pennies and started to walk out of the old building with his nickel.

Another man reportedly yelled after Bailey, accusing him of cheating. Bailey reportedly told the man he was going home and told the man where he could go himself. Then he kept on walking, but not for long.

Bailey was shot point-blank in the back with a .38 pistol.

I had chopped cotton beside T. B. Bailey and had gotten to know him the way folks do when they're working so close to the ground, their faces almost touch it. I'd heard Bailey talk about his slave ancestors and had sat fascinated by his other yarns as he broke bread with my family.

To this day I can see his dead eyes, staring open and blank into the sky.

Every black man in that smoky poker room knew who had shot T. B. Bailey. Not one would tell the white sheriff or Bailey's white employer.

My dad and I lifted up Bailey's body from where it had fallen, and some black folks took it away in a mule-drawn wagon. It has long since decayed in an unmarked grave no one will ever find under years of fallen leaves, deep in the Alabama woods. Bailey and his secrets are committed to the ground forever.

The sheriff's investigation, I'm told, consisted of one question posed to those who had witnessed the slaying.

"Which of you niggers done killed the dead nigger?" the sheriff supposedly said. His question was met with silence; his case was closed forever. Bailey was just one more illiterate black man laid to rest in the earth he lived to work until he died.

I had a lot of questions about the death of a man who had been under my roof and a part of my life. Each question was met with one answer: "Don't ask no questions, Tom."

And so I didn't. If I had, I would have met the same punishment handed to those who talked in class—a beating. That was the simple consequence for whispering in class— or talking openly about a black man's murder.

ANN AND I were going to a movie one night in Lafayette, Alabama, when I was about nineteen. I was driving that first car.

Suddenly, I was blinded by headlights approaching me in my lane. Officers later set the driver's speed at seventy-five miles per hour.

I hurled my car off the road, but not in time to avoid a head-on collision. The entire driver's side of the car was removed and I was temporarily pinned to the steering wheel. My leg was numb and without movement.

I didn't know that a piece of glass had gone across the top of my scalp, shaving it. I literally had a one-inch gap in my hair for weeks.

I sat there, bleeding, as Ann tried to free me from behind the wheel. I could see the fear on her face. She was concerned about her own condition, of which she was uncertain, but more concerned about mine. Her face was a mask of compassion.

In this life, one will notice love when it is least expected and most needed. Ann's was needed in the car that had hit us.

A young man, his wife, and baby were in that vehicle. The man, who was driving, was drunk. Ann worked to free me from our wreckage, and she walked as I stumbled to the aggressive car.

We watched the young man die, and then we watched his child die too. Neither of us had ever seen human death in process. Ann tried to get to each of its victims so she could hold them in her arms.

For weeks afterward, neither of us could get that young man and his four-year-old son out of our minds. I had nightmares.

The driver's arm had been amputated to the shoulder. Blood spewed from his torso. It ran across the front seat faster than fabric could absorb it. The young man screamed and begged God to let him live, and pleaded just as desperately for the life of his child. His eyes, and those of his child, slowly closed and never opened again.

But seeing death take such young and vibrant lives, who panicked as they knew they were passing, was something I'd like to forget but never will. I learned a valuable lesson from that incident. Things happen because we all must live, or die, with the consequences of our actions. They say every action breeds a reaction. That young man, probably an honest and hardworking fellow, had tried to cheat a law of the human race, the one that says alcohol impairs, and that those who abuse it shouldn't drive. I blame alcohol entirely for those two deaths that almost prompted two more.

I don't drink, but I don't condemn those who do. But from that day to this, I've never understood why people drink and drive. They wouldn't drive while blindfolded. Why do they drive when their senses are impaired, almost to the point of blindness, by alcohol?

I also learned something else from that tragedy: I'll never learn the answer to some questions. Never.


ANN AND I were married before the preacher and his wife. There were no other guests, as I didn't have the money to be able to afford them. The price of cake and punch was out of the question.

Our first night as man and wife was spent at the first motel we could find, about twenty miles from the preacher's house. Ann, to this day, accuses me of having gone duck hunting on the first day of our honeymoon. That isn't true. It was the second day.

My first child, Tommy, was born eighteen months after Ann and I were married. I wanted to reminisce about that, and my courtship of Ann, before I began to write these words. So I drove along the tree-lined dirt roads we'd traveled when we were young.

I drove over Flat Rock Road, made entirely of rocks that had been beneath the Alabama soil around Ann's house. The heavy rocks were yanked from the ground with the help of mules, then hauled by horse-drawn wagons. I drove to our old schoolhouse and walked through all the classrooms. I ran into old men I hadn't seen since they were young boys.

I've been all over the world. They've never been out of Penton. I've seen it all. They've seen peace of mind. I wondered whose vision had been best.

I spent the day strolling through fields, along trails, at my first fishing spot and around the church house where my family and I often joined others for dinner on the grounds. Everybody brought a covered dish to share with everybody else at those gatherings. Families sat beside other families on homemade quilts, eating chicken the farm wives had fried before daylight while a pie they'd made from scratch baked in a woodstove.

Those sleepy Sunday afternoons, the children played with balls or kites, while the grown-ups clapped along as four men sang old hymns in harmony, the origin of Southern gospel quartet music.

It was all as pure as something out of *The Waltons*.

My trip down memory lane ended at my old home place. The house was gone, absent, as if it had never been there. The soft purr of a light breeze was empty compared with the sound of laughing children heard fifty years earlier.

A house made of man's mortar and the land's rocks had been blown into blue sky. The old place, which my dad had sold years earlier, had been rented by two strangers from town. Nobody could believe the young men wanted to rent the abandoned house, whose sole occupants for years had been snakes and rats.

It seems the young men had no interest in the Mann family homestead itself. They wanted it not for history but for a hideout. They covered the windows with heavy curtains as if they feared being seen, even deep in the Alabama thicket. Very few people still lived in Penton, and Penton was a few miles away.

It may have been a hunter who happened on the house—or, rather, its remains. The sheriff came from the county seat, then used his two-way radio to call for an ambulance.

According to his report, the house had been converted into a lab for the manufacture of methamphetamines, a drug made with explosives. They ignited, killing the two men who made the drug and wiping out my old home place and any trace of the ten Manns who once lived there.

Today, if anyone should happen on the site, he'd find only a rock chimney standing above a rock fireplace. With no other sign of settlement, he'd have to wonder why a solitary rock pole rises twenty feet into the open sky.

He'd have no idea that it's a singular monument to ten Manns, one of whose life took him far beyond the shadow cast by the hand-stacked stones.

# CHAPTER SIX

I HADN'T BEEN a father for very long when I took a full-time job as a salesman at a hardware store in Shawmut, Alabama. I had worked there part-time after having recently graduated from high school.

I liked it because I got to sell a lot of fishing tackle and analyze lures whose designs I was sure I could improve upon. The lures were made on lathes and other machines. I carved mine by hand from wood and put the wood into a mold. I'd fill the mold with lead that I melted on a gas stove.

I designed the lures the same way I do today—at night, when I couldn't sleep. I kept a notepad by my bed stand, as I do to this day. If I awakened with thoughts of a lure's profile, I'd draw it in pencil.

I didn't know in 1950 that I'd enact that scenario more than 3,600 times, more than anyone else in the world, or that someday my lures would be mass-produced.

I liked the work at the hardware store because I could spend my off time fishing. I eventually worked at the cotton mill in Shawmut in the maintenance department. Later, I became a security guard at the mill.

Now, that job was a fisherman's dream.

I worked from eleven P.M. until seven A.M. I went home to sleep, then went fishing every afternoon before reporting to work that night.

Ann and I had lived with her parents for a few months immediately after getting married but now had our own little place in town. She, too, worked at the cotton mill, but on a different shift.

I spent much of my time at work sitting at a desk tying the lures I had designed. I made them mostly for myself but decided to try to sell a few to my friends and neighbors.

What would one day become a multi-million-dollar business was interrupted by two cents worth of postage.

"Greetings!" the notice began.

To American boys over age eighteen, that was the most dreaded word in the English language. I had been drafted.

I left Ann with Tommy, still in diapers, and pregnant with Sharon, who'd be born before I was discharged.

I hated the army. It promised to make me a man, but a male who's supporting a family on a cotton mill salary is already a man. And there was the matter of unnecessary discipline. I didn't like to be told what to do. Sergeants were telling me how to shoot a rifle when I could shoot off a gnat's wings at forty yards. I've spent most of my life working for myself because I don't welcome orders from others unless they're qualified people. That's not to say that I don't appreciate how much the United States military—and those who've served in it—have done for this country. But more about that later.

I rode a bus with three of my buddies to Fort Jackson, South Carolina. Once there, we disembarked to the sound of a drill sergeant yelling insults so loudly, his neck veins bulged. We hadn't even had time to make him angry. He was just naturally mad at the world, as we'd soon learn.

One time, for example, we were made to stand in formation while the sergeant yelled hysterically because our barracks weren't clean enough to suit him. The floor shone and everything was in its place. The placement of our soap and toothbrushes had been precisely measured with rulers to be sure they were exactly where they were supposed to be in our footlockers. I thought the barracks looked like a military museum. If the sergeant thought it was dirty, I wondered what he'd have thought about my old home place, where the wind blew through the cracks in the walls.

We had worked for hours, often on our hands and knees, to meet the standards of his inspection. No matter.

"The barracks is a shit hole" he yelled. I thought his opinion was exaggerated and that he might have mistakenly gone through another barracks. He did not, however, seem interested in reconsidering his assessment.

"You sons of bitches get back in there and clean that shit hole," he thundered.

"Clean it your damn self," someone in the ranks muttered.

"Who said that?" the sergeant demanded. "Who said that?"

The sergeant was out of his mind with rage. I thought about suggesting there had been a misunderstanding, but something told me my suggestion would not be well taken.

No one admitted to having told the sergeant to clean his own barracks. So the sergeant said that if the guilty man wouldn't tell on himself, perhaps another trainee would tell on him. He announced that the entire platoon could think about that as it stood at rigid attention, in formation, in ninety-five-degree heat.

Our training uniforms had long-sleeve shirts made of extremely heavy cotton. The uniforms were about six sizes too large, so as to humiliate the trainees. All of us looked like Andy Gump in army green. And the baggy material trapped the heat like a sauna.

We stood there for so long that boys began to faint from dehydration. We were supposedly being trained to fight the North Koreans. I didn't see how the cleanliness of our barracks would help us do that. Were we supposed to assault the Communists with laundry detergent? I didn't get it.

Hours later, after several men had been revived with a helmet full of cold water dashed in their face, the man who'd suggested that the sergeant do housework confessed.

"By God!" a voice rang from the back of the platoon. "I said it!"

The barracks held 150 boys/men. That sergeant made the guilty boy clean its entire floor with soap, water, and a toothbrush. The trainee wore holes in the knees of his uniform and blisters on his palms. He also wore out twenty toothbrushes.

I got it: We were being trained to attack the North Koreans with toothbrushes! Our heavy artillery would be vegetable brushes.

The sergeant awoke us every morning at three A.M. by walking through the barracks banging a club against the lid of a metal garbage can. I wondered if he knew that in a group that large, the odds were that some folks would be at their best if awakened gradually. Something told me to keep that notion to myself too.

More and more, the army made less and less sense to me.

Our sergeants, I decided, clearly needed a friend. Maybe the informal approach would enable us to bond.

I had just walked into the supply room to be issued my first rifle, when I noticed it was without a combination tool. I thought I could best point out the oversight by approaching the master sergeant informally. He had military stripes that lined the arms of his fatigues. He looked like a zebra in cotton.

"Hey, Sarge," I said, knowing he'd notice that I hadn't addressed him as sergeant. I was sure he was tired of hearing that word. "My rifle hasn't got a combination—"

That's as far as I got.

"Hey, boy," he said, "you know the best way to get a combination tool?"

"Why, no, I don't," I said, thinking his response might be a step toward friendship.

"You back out the door and shit one!"

Instantly, I knew that he didn't want to be buddies.

I had been taught I should be kind to other folks, and

they should be kind to me. I hadn't been off our family farm and its protectiveness long enough to become insensitive. I had sincerely reached out to the sergeant, I had thought, and he had insulted and embarrassed me in front of the other trainees.

I went back to the barracks, my feelings deeply hurt, worrying about how I'd get a combination tool. I knew I couldn't pass inspection without one.

What occurred next marked the first time I'd ever bucked unnecessary authority. Some folks are mean just because they have the power to be, I thought.

So I announced to every trainee in the barracks that our sergeant was giving away free combination tools for rifles and that we could each take one home when we got our first furlough.

There was a run on the place. One hundred and fifty men ran thundering, looking like a herd of elephants zoning in on the human zebra. The sergeant was not amused. He wanted to know who had told them they could get souvenir combination tools. No one could say, since we hadn't had time yet to learn each other's names. All each man could say was some guy with a shaved head in an army training uniform had shouted it to the barracks. They said his face was hard to see, and it was. My oversize cap hid my face.

Their description fit me and 149 others.

I was never caught.

I eventually got through basic training and was enrolled in demolition school. I was trained to disarm land mines and other bombs. In a company of almost three hundred men, all but seven were sent to Korea, where they participated in hand-to-hand combat.

All returned—many in body bags.

I CAME OUT of the service and resumed work at the cotton mill, which had a curious system of internal economics. The same company that owned the mill also owned most of the houses and nearby grocery stores. I therefore spent my mill paycheck buying the mill's groceries and paying the mill rent.

The system reminded me of the army's. There, a married man could use his government pay to shop at government stores and rent a government-owned house.

Ann, the kids, and I decided I would augment my cotton-mill income by beefing up my old trapping practice and raising wildlife.

That's right. Shawmut was not exactly a bustling metropolis. But it wasn't the kind of rural area I'd grown up either. This was a town of tidy suburban homes with mowed grass and painted shutters. In the middle of it all, it had rabbits that bred constantly and roosters that seemingly crowed nonstop.

Not until the 1960s would network television produce a show called *The Beverly Hillbillies*, a comedy about the Clampett family, mountain folks who brought their rural ways to the city.

Ann, my kids, and I were ahead of our time. You've heard about the hayseed who goes to Rome? We were the Manns come to Shawmut.

When I was a boy, the first thing a farmer did when he moved onto land was clear it. I carried on the tradition. Our little suburban bungalow was shaded by beautiful hundred-year-old pine trees—until I cut them down.

I watched the neighbors watching me, standing in their yards and shaking their heads. Their yards were manicured. Mine was an enormous log pile.

Then I built the rabbit house. It was an eyesore but home to the thirteen does and one buck I had as seed animals. I had seventy-five baby rabbits in about a month.

The first day I put the buck in with those does he was romantic with each of them—one after the other. He made the females baby-making machines. The way he was siring rabbits, I was sure I'd be rich in no time simply by selling my game in a town where the company store sold and processed meat.

So I decided to expand my empire to quail. They fluttered and pooped on my yard and the neighbors' roofs before flapping into their brooder house at night to roost.

The neighbors complained about the chickens squawking, but I thought that was just because they were jealous of all the money I was going to make.

By then my rooster had become psychotic. He crowed without stopping, and my neighbors prayed without ceasing. I wondered if roosters could get hoarse.

"Keep that bird quiet!" my neighbors yelled through raised windows.

"I can't hear you!" I yelled. "The rooster is crowing too loud."

This went on for weeks. My power saw roared as it cut the fallen trees into logs; the animals bellowed because that's what animals do.

Then came the day of the slaughter.

Chicken feathers sifted across green lawns in July like snowfall in January. It almost never snows in Alabama, not in January or any other time. Snowfall would have been pretty on the neighbors' lawns. They didn't feel that way about chicken feathers.

I had pounds and pounds, probably hundreds of pounds, of chicken, rabbit, and quail meat for sale. I hung out a sign and I started walking door-to-door.

A guy with a badge one day came out of nowhere and asked to see my license.

"What license?" I asked.

"The one that entitles you to have this meat inspected by the government," he said. "By the way, where is your inspection stamp?"

I had no idea what he was talking about. On the farm, we had grown and eaten our own food without government interference. Not so in town. I had built animal houses, bought animal food, alienated all of my neighbors, and slaughtered scores of animals with no knowledge that I was supposed to be doing so under government supervision that had to culminate with a meat inspection stamp.

The man told me that if I sold one ounce of my meat, I'd be arrested.

For a long time after that, Ann didn't buy meat at the company store. We ate every chicken, rabbit, and quail ourselves—for more than a year. We had meat three times a day.

Some of the mill workers didn't know about my sideline business.

"How much money do you earn at the mill?" they asked. "Me and my old lady cain't hardly afford chitlins, and you're eating meat for every meal. How do you do it?"

"Buy the meat when it's young," I said.

"Huh?" they said.

Then I'd open my lunch bucket and chow down on a cold rabbit leg or quail's breast.

You can take the Mann out of the country, but you can't take the country out of the Mann. I've proven that too.

I ENDURED MY job at the mill, looked at the ruins of my residential lot, and tied my lures on and off the company clock. Ann and the kids did the same, and before long I was selling them to coworkers at the mill and around Shawmut at gasoline stations.

In the 1950s South, every gas station sold fishing tackle. So did every hardware and sporting goods store.

A lot of folks around Shawmut knew me because I frequently gave away fish at the mill. A lot of the guys asked to go fishing with me, and they marveled at what I could catch on homemade lures.

The mill had a pond on its grounds. I caught fish elsewhere, then snuck them into the pond at night. In no time the big fish I'd put in there gave birth to little fish, and the pond teemed with life.

I tested many of my lures in the company pond on company time. As a security guard, I was supposed to punch a time clock at various parts of the plant to show that I was making my rounds. I'd punch the clock, fish for an hour by dark of night, then go to the appropriate place to punch a clock again.

Guys who worked other jobs would work fast to get ahead on their production quotas. Then they'd meet me at the pond, and we'd fish. One guy came right after I punched my midnight clock, another after I punched my one A.M. clock, another after the two A.M. clock, and so forth until daylight.

I showed those guys how to cast for fish and how to clean them. All my services were free, and that cultivated a market for the one thing that wasn't—my lures. They were for sale.

By then I was earning about fifty dollars a week guarding the Shawmut cotton mill in Shawmut.

I was earning about ten times that much selling the mill's workers fishing lures. My hobby had become a business, and business was good.

My life was becoming that way too.

# CHAPTER SEVEN

I CONTINUED MAKING lures at home and running my sales route around Southeast Alabama. I eventually employed about five housewives, plus Ann, who oversaw the hand-painting of the lures and kept the financial records. Those women were able to produce as many lures as I could sell to area retailers when not working at the cotton mill.

Mann Bait Co. was founded in 1958 with a five dollar investment, the living room assembly line, and priceless support from my family.

My kids—Tommy, Sharon, Cindy, and Nelda, put the lures into bags. I drove to little towns near my Alabama home to hang my lures at gas stations, where signs read TOM MANN'S HANDMADE LURES FOR SALE.

After forty-two years and the sale of one billion lures, I'm still selling bait that bears my name. But I'll never forget my fledgling business, when a dollar was about as certain as my next meal. When the customers didn't immediately come to me, I decided to go to them.

I surmised that people didn't merely want to hear that my lures were good; they wanted to see it for themselves.

Show them and sell them, I decided. That was the thinking behind what was actually an infomercial before anyone had heard the word. Only I didn't make my presentation on television; I made it in person.

I drove to Florida with a cigar box filled with Sting Ray Grubs, one of the first grubs I invented.

There were no Wal-Marts, K marts or Targets in 1958. Sears hadn't heard of Tom Mann. What became the biggest retail bonanza of my charter year was orchestrated by me, one man who spent one afternoon on one beach.

I initially attracted little attention as I strolled the glistening Florida sand. People were preoccupied with a busy school of amberjack in the clear water beneath the pier where I eventually stood, ignored. I tried to hawk my wares, but my polite pitch was lost in the chatter of excited people viewing the fish.

If I caught one of those fish with one of my lures, I'd catch business from the frustrated fishermen lining the pier, I decided.

I had not done that much saltwater fishing in those days. I wanted to think like the fish below, but couldn't until I watched them. I noticed that they were finicky eaters, dismissing all food—real or artificial—except for the sand fleas that occasionally hopped from the ocean floor en route to the surface. Again, I noted that a school of fish is like a classroom filled with children: When one has something, the others want it. An amberjack that hit one flea would himself be hit by other amberjack who wanted his catch.

"Let me think this through," I said to myself. "What lure would I hit if I were an amberjack?" The answer was obvious: an artificial sand flea.

I had no fake fleas.

I decided to improvise and give the amberjack what they thought they wanted.

I dropped my Sting Ray Grub and let it sink slowly on a line to the bottom. The amberjack didn't notice. I let the grub lie so the tide-pushed sand would soon cover it.

When I figured the lure was buried under two inches of sand, I jerked it hard from the bottom. Real sand fleas make a tiny cloud of dust when they dart from beneath the water. I decided mine would make a giant dust bowl, like something from an underwater version of *The Grapes of Wrath*. The Superman of sand fleas bolted into a school of swimming amberjack. I had often put "skirts" on my lures. I should have given that grub a cape.

One amberjack furiously struck the aggressive lure. As soon as he hit, the others hit him to steal his prey.

Meanwhile, my fish pulled my line like a block and tackle with gills. A two-pound amberjack fights with more power than a ten-pound bass. It was fishing at its pole-bending best.

The other amberjack continued to swirl around my one fish with "food," their swaying tails making a small but visible swell in the water's surface.

Up and down the beach, people began to yell "amber-jack!" They acted like the fish they'd been seeking. Everyone wanted what another, me, already had. They began to buy from my cigar box of Sting Ray Grubs.

I held my pole in one hand while I made change with the other. I had created a frenzy both below and above the water.

At that point, the amberjack were so excited and competitive, they would hit any lure dropped into the water. Luckily, the fishermen were dropping mine. Then, as quickly as it started, it stopped. Each fish in the school of perhaps fifty had followed the others in taking a shot at "food." They bit no more.

I had a few lures left and decided to try the same trick again. Fish have short memories, very short. People who say they can't catch fish because the fish have been hooked by their lures before are wrong.

I again dropped the lure to the water's floor and waited for the sand to cover it. Then I again ripped it from the sea bottom. Again, an amberjack instantly hit my line, and people again lined up to buy my lures.

I sold out.

My trick of tricking the amberjack had paid off. I left the pier with a pocket bulging with cash. A business started on five dollars had made its first hundred.

MY LURE BUSINESS seemed to accelerate after that, although I'm not suggesting what happened with the Florida amberjack had anything to do with its significant expansion.

Ann began to have all kinds of notions about the business, and as early as 1959 toyed with the idea of a mail order catalog. But it was too early. I had not yet turned professional fisherman and, in fact, had no thoughts of it. Eight-hundred numbers weren't common, if they were even existent, and of course, there was no such thing as home computers, much less the Internet. We would one day use each of those forums.

In the meantime, we grew rapidly and solidly thanks to the most effective sales tool of all—word of mouth. People in the little towns around Southeast Alabama knew Tom Mann and Mann Bait Co.

Word had gotten out that I designed my lures with a pencil and paper, carved a likeness from the drawing out of wood with a pocket knife, made a mold to fit the likeness, and filled the mold with hot lead. The lead lure was then adorned with hooks and hand-painted. People were intrigued by our cottage industry, as folks in the late 1950s still enjoyed a craft that was performed by a craftsman, not a machine. They liked the personal touch and liked to think they knew the person behind it.

But I was restless.

I'd had a quiet ambition all of my life that I had shared with very few people: I wanted to be a game warden. I loved animals and felt strongly about conservation. I hated the abuse of hunting and fishing laws. Wildlife had given me more pleasurable hours than anything other than my family. I wanted to give something back. I wanted to help protect the creatures, great and small, that had been my emotional and physical sustenance.

My second love was the out-of-doors. Protecting wildlife in its natural habitat was a job description for game warden. It was as if the job had been created with me in mind.

I applied to the Alabama Department of Conservation, and in 1960 I became Officer Tom Mann.

I couldn't believe I got paid for doing what I loved—being outdoors whenever I wanted and wherever I wanted (within my jurisdiction).

A person should become a police officer primarily because he wants to help people, not because he wants to make arrests or abuse authority. A person should become a game warden because he wants to help wildlife. I was in the right job for the right reason.

I didn't believe in showing favorites or looking the other way. I put personal preferences aside and enforced the law and only the law, and I enforced it by the book.

People have no idea how much wildlife is spared because of conservation officers. A man who's willing to get up at three A.M. and hide amid brush in freezing water to police a duck hunter's limit does so because he believes in protecting creatures that often can't protect themselves. He's not out there because he wants to write someone a ticket. If that's all he wanted, he could be a parking meter attendant, enjoying normal hours and standing on solid ground and taking breaks in central heat or air-conditioning. Hunters and fishermen owe much to the men and women who ensure that wildlife will prosper from generation to generation. After all, most animals' biggest predator is man, and man is greedy.

If not for conservation laws, and those who enforce them, the world would be devoid of wildlife in no time. The endangered species list would be as long as a list of lottery contestants.

In the 1950s and '60s, however, game wardens were

thought of as cops of the wilderness. A lot of people don't like the folks in law enforcement, and that dislike sometimes extended to game wardens. The results were sometimes tragic and sometimes hilarious.

A guy once tried to outrun me in his automobile during a high-speed chase. When I caught up with him, he was shooting into a treetop in July, two months before the start of squirrel season. I didn't have to be Sherlock Holmes to deduce that he was squirrel hunting illegally.

At his hearing, he told the justice of the peace I had no grounds for arresting him.

"This here game warden thought I was a hunting squirrels when I was a shootin' into the trees," he argued. "I was a-huntin' my hogs."

There was a long silence while the magistrate sat in disbelief.

"How many hogs did you kill in the treetop?" he asked.

"Well, sir, I, I . . ." the defendant stammered in a vain attempt to answer the question. He was fined ten dollars plus two dollars in court costs. He could have bought a lot of squirrel meat with that money forty years ago.

I learned to be a game warden while training with a senior officer. He called himself an old dog and told me that my watching him would teach me how to hunt. He was right.

We once came upon two fishermen whose poles were resting on the ground. He explained that we could not ask to see their licenses until we had seen them actually fish.

When they at last picked up their poles, we approached and found them staggering drunk.

The older man, the other's father, said he had not known

we were near until he spotted our uniforms. In other words, he wouldn't have fished had he known we were watching.

My partner asked to see his fishing license.

"Let's see *your* fishing license," the suspect said smartly.

"I'm not fishing," my mentor said.

"I ain't either," said the old drunk.

"I'll ask you once more to please see your license," the game warden said.

"I'll ask you once more to see *yours*," the drunk replied.

That was it. My partner was mad. He told me to open the back door to our car. I did, whereupon he threw the old drunk onto the seat, belly first. When the old fisherman's son objected, he threw the boy on top of his dad.

The boy began to whine.

"Daddy, what are they going to do to us?" the boy asked.

"Shut up, son," the drunk said. "They're going to kill us."

The arresting officer told the judge of the drunk's crack about being executed for fishing without a license. The judge was not amused. He found each defendant guilty, then sentenced them to death.

"Just kidding," the judge said right before the whining boy fainted.

Father and son were each slapped with a twelve-dollar fine, including court costs.

There was a lawlessness that pervaded rural Alabama almost a half century ago. Moonshine stills were common. Families still lived in cabins with children who weren't always enrolled in school. What today is politely called domestic violence was then accurately called wife beating. It went on routinely behind closed doors in the dark woods of the Deep South.

Some say the South was America's last frontier. I don't know about that. But there was frontier justice.

All the wardens I knew wanted to be taken seriously, as they were serious about conservation. That was sometimes difficult among suspects I considered personal friends. It was awkward to shake down a suspect whose kids went to school with mine or whose wife attended the same church as mine.

To deal with this, I consciously set aside friendship when I wore a uniform.

I guess my friend, who I'll call Tim, was having the same thoughts the day he thought he was making a routine approach for a routine hunting license check involving an old buddy. Tim, I'm sure, was characteristically outgoing when he walked up on our friend—and a woman.

Adultery was the height of scandal in backwoods Alabama more than forty years ago. Tim caught our mutual friend in a sexual act with another man's wife. We'd been taught to never make an arrest without carrying a pistol. But perhaps because he had recognized his buddy, Tim walked up without his firearm. Or maybe Tim was just negligent. He had been watching the guy, who appeared to be hunting, from his cruiser.

The adulterous man, who'd known Tim longer than I had, panicked. Maybe he saw his life as a husband and father going down the tubes. Maybe he couldn't live with what would have been unthinkable shame. Maybe he just wasn't thinking—period.

The woman testified that although the defendant assured Tim he was reaching for his hunting license, he was actually going for his knife. He stabbed Tim to death, and then he stabbed him again and again. Out of his mind, he used the knife, sufficient to clean a deer, to decapitate Tim.

His head was found at the site of what might have been a misdemeanor violation for hunting without a license.

The adulterer was sentenced to die, exhausted all of his appeals, and was electrocuted. The district attorney had established premeditation after the woman testified that Tim had spent his last minutes on earth begging for his life.

Being a game warden is, in a way, the most dangerous of all police work. In any other arena of law enforcement, an officer is entitled to shoot a suspect who is brandishing a gun. A game warden routinely walks alone, carrying a solitary pistol tucked into a holster, into a group of men toting shotguns or high-powered rifles that are sometimes cocked and shouldered.

The mere twitching of a trigger is all that separates the game warden from life and death, usually in a remote area where there are no witnesses. The site of the killing is almost always devoid of fingerprints, which can't be lifted from trees or other plant growth.

Other law enforcement officers make arrests in cities or along traveled roads, often after calling for backup. The game warden makes his arrests by himself.

Game wardens risk their lives to protect animal life.

The second lesson we were taught as would-be game wardens was to write a suspect's automobile tab number on the palm of our hands before approaching a vehicle.

Another of my game warden friends learned that lesson well.

Tipped to their presence by a car parked along the road, he approached some guys with shotguns who'd gathered in a dove field. Dove hunters usually hunt in groups. The hunters didn't know the game warden had written down their car's tag number on his hand. He didn't know they were only pretending to be hunters and were, in fact, making a major drug transaction.

"How ya all doin' this mornin'?" the game warden said.

Those were his last words, we'd later learn.

He was shot, almost in two, by shotgun blasts.

I was dispatched to the scene with the most dreaded words known to those in law enforcement: "Officer down!"

I arrived at the remote crime scene about the same time as other game wardens and members of the Alabama Highway Patrol.

You see a lot of sights in the wilderness. I know it's simply survival of the fittest, but I still can't get hardened to the sight of an alligator devouring a fawn, so new to this world that he or she staggers, then cries while eaten alive. I could never get jaded to some things, natural or not.

Similarly, if I had stayed in conservation for the rest of my life, I could have never gotten used to the sight of a fellow game warden lying in a pool of his own blood.

I was the first warden to approach our dead colleague. Law enforcement personnel would later string crime-scene tape around the body, as if that would protect it. The lawmen would mutter and try to look at the body while unavoidably looking away.

I leaned over my dead friend and opened his palm. I used water from a canteen to rinse away his blood. There, on his hand, was an automobile tag number.

We ran a trace and arrested the suspects in a matter of hours.

Two of the men are in the penitentiary to this day.

I had serious misgivings after that. Was my fantasy job as a game warden worth my life and my kids' future? Was I really doing this because I loved animal life, or because I loved to be its protector? Was I a savior to the animals, or serving myself?

My lure business continued to grow. I earned fifty dollars a week as a game warden. I was earning five hundred, after paying the employees working in my basement, helping me make and distribute lures.

Quitting the job to enhance a career seemed to be the obvious thing to do. However I looked at it, I knew that I was directly or indirectly earning my living from wildlife, the same wildlife that had given me years of pleasure as a lad—and a livelihood as an adult and provider.

Despite my misgivings, I had to give something back, at least for a while longer. I stayed in conservation.

I knew that being safe, and working at home, were not the same thing. I'd had an eye-opening experience in my basement during my stint as a game warden.

I was making lures, pouring molten lead through a metal pipe into a metal mold. A lightning storm was under way outside.

I actually heard the lightning, for a split second, before I felt it inside my basement. I know that it's a cliché to say that it was as loud as a freight train. But the lightning was as loud as a freight train as it shot through the lead infrastructure of my modest house.

It leapt from a vertical pipe and hit the lead mold in my hand. I was literally lifted off my feet and thrown backward. I don't know if I've ever been hit harder, but I know I've never been hit harder and retained consciousness.

Some of my teeth were loosened.

The hot and melted plastic for the worm mold was splattered onto the walls and ceiling. The scalding stuff went all over me. I lay on the basement floor in a haze, wondering what happened, who I was, and what I'd been doing.

I've never felt such force.

I simply rested awhile, then struggled to my feet and the process of cleaning up the mess. I'd had another of what would become many near death experiences, and I hadn't gone beyond the safety of my home workbench. I hadn't even gone above ground.

The safety of the home became a myth to me then. Sometimes that myth recurs to this day, especially when I think about crime and how it touches residential America.

In the field, as a game warden, I once pulled my boat alongside a fisherman who was catching bass with a speckled plastic worm. It looked amazingly like the Jelly Worm I had designed, a lure that would go on to become the most popular plastic worm I ever made. I've sold untold millions.

By this time Mann Bait Co. had been moved from my basement into a little plant in Eufaula, Alabama, the town where I live today. The move had nothing to do with the lightning strike.

I asked the guy where he got the plastic worm the bass were hitting so rapidly. He told me that it was made by

Mann Bait Co., and that he had a female friend who worked there. He said she stole at least a thousand of the lures over a period of time, then he offered me some of my own creations free of charge. He had no idea he was talking to the president of the company from which his girlfriend was stealing.

I returned to the plant, confronted her, and accepted her admission. She wanted me to accept her resignation, but I couldn't. I'd already fired her.

I can't stand a thief.

Had she been stealing to feed her kids or something equally important, I might have reconsidered. But she was stealing to give them to her stupid boyfriend, who didn't know he'd tattled on her to her boss.

I think a lot of people feel that game wardens have no right to police the bagging of creatures put on this earth by God. They forget that conservation helps ensure the birth of those fish and animals.

A landowner once told me that no game warden owned the doves that flew over his land. He said that he owned them. Who owned them after they flew off his land? I asked. He argued, but couldn't answer.

A third shooting incident was the last straw for me. It also involved a game warden friend.

When the warden asked to see a man's license, the man responded by shoving his shotgun barrel under the officer's nose. Then he threatened to pull the trigger.

The man's son ran to him, begging him to spare the officer's life. The hillbilly hunter, perhaps drunk or desperate for food, dropped his shotgun to slap the boy. When his gun hit the ground, the warden pulled his pistol.

He could have shot the man but instead ordered him to put his hands in the air. The suspect responded by pulling a sidearm and firing. The warden, who wasn't hit, went down intentionally. As he did, he fired a .45 bullet into the suspect's stomach. A .45 is a big, slow slug the United States military used from World War II and the Korean conflict to the Vietnam War and Operation Desert Storm.

The suspect reeled and raised his pistol to shoot at the warden again. The warden rolled over and fired again. He rolled a total of six times and fired six rounds.

It was straight out of a John Wayne movie, except it wasn't acting—it was a real-life drama that eventually changed my path. I loved the job, but I hated its risks and their threat to my family. I feared that my luck might run out.

I resigned from the Alabama Department of Conservation.

One relative had a fit.

"You got a job that's paying you fifty dollars a week," the relative said. "You've got a family to think of. You need to know that you're going to get a paycheck every Friday, not some big check from selling fish bait that might be here one week and not be here the next.

"You got to think about that steady check that will come every Friday."

"How do I know I'll live from Friday to Friday?" I asked.

With that, the relative, like the state of Alabama, accepted my resignation.

# CHAPTER EIGHT

I HAVE UNDERSTATED the growth of the Mann Bait Co. due to hands-on involvement during my six years as a game warden.

I made the point that a game warden spends a lot of time secretly watching suspects. He may wait for hours before he sees someone catch a fish that exceeds the limit, or kill an animal out of season.

I confess that I spent much of that idle time hand-tying lures. I tied polar-bear hair, for example, to jigs and to hooks because I enjoyed it, and because I wanted to keep my personal touch on my growing business.

The popularity of my business was, in fact, exploding.

It's amazing how many hundreds of lures a dozen people can create during a day through mass production. One person pours plastic or lead into a mold, another retrieves it from the mold, another spray-paints the lure, another spray-paints another part another color, another paints still another part still another color, another paints the eyes, another attaches the hooks, and another puts them into boxes. People were doing all of that inside my garage.

I'm simplifying the process, of course. But mass-producing products that weigh a few ounces or less is much easier than mass-producing heavy equipment that must be moved on sturdy conveyor belts and by hydraulic lifts.

I'd eventually have as many as seven hundred employees working simultaneously in mass production for my various companies. Our conveyor was usually no more than a bicycle chain moved by electricity. Lures dangled from the chain.

Mass-producing lures requires no heavy lifting, and no "skilled" labor. Laborers can be taught their jobs in a few hours, and usually can perform them to perfection in a few days.

The "skill" in lure production comes in lure design, whose idea usually comes to me when I least expect it. Then, as now, I often awakened with a pattern in my mind. Or the idea for a lure came as I walked the street or drove a car. I have drawn lures minutes after awakening from a sound sleep, or while driving with one hand and drawing with the other.

I went to Birmingham, Alabama, in the middle 1960s to present my line of lures to executives at Kmart. They bought them. In fact, they put Mann Bait Co. lures into every Kmart in that district. The lures sold well, and soon I was in every Kmart in Alabama.

A year later, I was in every Kmart in the nation.

I soon rented a building, hired more people, and produced more lures.

Today, lures are sold on consignment. A distributor buys them from the manufacturer and sells them to a retailer. The retailer returns to the distributor whatever lures he fails to sell, and the distributor returns them to the manufacturer. Today, no sale of a lure by a manufacturer is actually final until it is sold by the retailer, or bought without the right of return by a national distributor.

In the 1960s, however, all sales by a manufacturer were final. If a retailer bought ten thousand of my lures, he paid for that many, and I knew exactly how much money I was making.

I never made more lures than I could sell. My difficulty lay in producing all the lures that were wanted by the retailers. I made lures that were runaway hits with fishermen, and that are still in production to this day, such as the Little George and the Jelly Worm.

I went from Kmart to other national chain retailers, and eventually would sell my lures in Wal-Mart, Sears, and Target stores, not to mention other retail outlets.

There was no Internet in those days, and I don't recall anyone using an 800 number. But people would write to me, and I composed a mailing list. I later published a catalog that was regularly sent to each correspondent.

I had started my business in my kitchen with a five-dollar investment and a mold carved with a pocket knife. A few years later, I was deriving an annual gross income in seven figures.

I've read where my lures were popular because I was a high-profile professional bass fisherman whose name was widely known among fishermen. That isn't true. I began to sell successfully lures long before I became a professional fisherman. My lures were popular because they were good lures. People associated good lures with Mann the way they associated good chocolate with Hershey.

I had not even entered, much less won, a national tournament when my lures began to catch hold among America's fishermen. But I was smart enough to put my photograph on the box that held the lures. I therefore became a household word among anglers in the United States and eventually overseas.

I would enter my first bass tournament in 1968 when Ray Scott, the president of BASS (Bass Anglers Sportsmen Society), called me. He told me he was going to sponsor a tournament, and that he hoped to build bass fishing to a nationally sanctioned event, which he eventually did. BASS today is to professional bass fishing what the National Football League is to professional football.

Today's tournaments pay their winners as much as $250,000, so obviously, some select fishermen follow the tournament trail. The very first BASS tournament paid $2,000, as I recall. I fished in it.

Scott is a former insurance salesman who is very magnetic and persuasive. He's a likable guy who could sell weeds to a sod farmer.

He called me and explained what he was going to do in

terms of promoting a bass fishing tournament, and how the tournament would be the first of what would become regularly scheduled national events. I thought his plans were ambitious, but I liked Ray. I considered entering his tournament as a favor to him.

"How much will it cost me to enter this tournament?" I asked.

"Only one hundred dollars," Scott replied.

"I don't know," I said, "I don't think I want to take the time off work, and I don't want to risk the hundred dollars."

"You should enter the tournament because you're sure to win it," Scott said. "The fact that you win the tournament by fishing with your own lures will help your lure business, especially as one tournament breeds another, and as I build this thing into national competition. Now, come on and enter this first tournament. Just between you and me, you're the best fisherman I've invited. You're sure to win the tournament."

I later found out that he had told one hundred other fishermen that they were the best, and that they were sure to win.

I laugh about that each time I look at the receipt for my hundred-dollar entry fee.

I finished my first tournament in fourth place.

I entered Ray's next tournament and finished in second place. I came in second place many times, and then I finally won four tournaments.

Each time I won one hundred dollars.

THE FIRST YEAR of national bass tournaments was finished with the Bass Masters Classic Tournament. The top
twenty-four fishermen in terms of point standings were invited to fish for the title of national champion.

I was the first runner-up in that tournament. I was its
leader for two days, then lost it on the last cast, thrown by
Bobby Murry. I lost ten thousand dollars, a sizable amount of
money at that time, and the title of national champion in a
matter of seconds.

Bobby Murry is a talented fisherman.

He was accompanied in his boat by outdoor writer
Charles Salter, who told me the following story.

Bobby had gone about twenty miles up the river and
knew that he'd have to sprint back to the finish line in order
to meet the competition deadline. If he'd have been late, he
would have been disqualified.

He started for the finish line and noticed a point, an arm
of land, on the river that he had never fished. He threw one
cast and caught one bass. It weighed slightly more than five
pounds. That's a nice tournament bass.

Bobby had not even turned off his trolling motor, I was
told. He simply threw, reeled, and headed for home.

Bobby was so pressed for time that he did not put his
catch in the live well, the tank within a bass boat where fish
are kept alive.

The outdoor writer lifted the fish from the boat's floor
and put him in the well as Bobby sped for the finish line. He
arrived with two minutes to spare.

I had caught twenty-eight bass, Bobby had caught seventeen. Bass tournaments are won by the contestant who

catches the most pounds of fish, not the highest number. The five-pounder had put Bobby a pound or so over the collective weight of my fish.

He won fair and square.

IT DIDN'T TAKE long for me to see the dark side of competition among likable men who'd formerly fished all of their lives purely for sport. Attaching a price tag to an event always changes the attitude of contestants.

After losing my first shot at the national championship, I was fishing in a tournament where I "read" the water and the weather as I still do today. I talked earlier about structure fishing, and I sought structure during practice rounds that preceded competitive rounds. I remember fishing once alongside a buoy, the only structure floating in several square miles of water.

Another tournament fisherman saw me by that structure. He saw how I was hoisting fish rapidly from the water. What he didn't know was that the buoy's value as structure was secondary. It happened to sit above an underwater ledge. Fish lie on top of "shelves" on the bottom of a lake or river. If you can find such a shelf, you'll usually find fish. Such shelves are found by the long process of letting your lure hit bottom to determine the depth. If your lure suddenly falls several feet deeper into the water without your moving your boat, you've likely found an underwater shelf. Bouncing your lure off the bottom in that area will help you determine the layout of the invisible shelf, a fishing bonanza.

The other tournament fisherman thought I was catching fish by the buoy simply because it was the only structure in the water.

The next day, when official competition began, I drove my boat to the buoy and the other tournament fisherman had already parked there. Sure enough, he was catching fish. They darted from the top of the ledge and hit his lure.

Again, he thought they were drawn to the buoy, and had no idea I had earlier fished beside the buoy because it was merely a marker for the shelf.

That night, on the eve of the second day of tournament competition, I secretly put my boat back into the water. Being sure that no one saw me, I drove my boat to the middle of the river and to the buoy. I attached a rope to the floating object.

I could hear the clang of steel against steel as the rope's hook was snapped into place on the buoy. Sounds on the water are loud at night, especially when one is trying to be silent and sneaky.

I pulled the buoy with a rope about a hundred yards away from its original mooring. My boat engine roared against the strain, and I feared someone would hear me out in the middle of the water. No one did.

The next day, the other fisherman got up early to race to his spot beside the buoy, not knowing he was as far as a football field is long from his former hot spot.

I pulled to the spot where the buoy had been, above the underwater shelf.

I slaughtered the fish, and won that day's competition.

I don't feel as though I stole the man's fishing spot. I merely reclaimed what he had stolen from me.

I won the four-day tournament. I spent my time reeling in fish; he spent his mindlessly rocking in a boat by a buoy.

Incidentally, I got the idea to tug the buoy because Ray had once fished a hole under a log that floated on Lake Eufaula. I had shown him the log. I later noticed through field glasses that he returned to the hot spot with guests and without me. One night, I pulled the floating log several yards from its usual spot. Ray fished for days afterward under the log's new resting place. He didn't know the log had been moved. He caught no fish, and was never the wiser until I told him.

WITH THE EXCEPTION of Ray, nobody made any significant money from those early regular season tournaments, whose primary sponsor was Ranger Boats. But they were valuable to me, as they bolstered my confidence as a fisherman. Ray was handpicking the men who he believed were the best fishermen in the nation, no matter what he had to say to draft them. I was holding my own with all of them, and surpassing most of them.

I believe in the importance of self-confidence to this day. If a boxer gets in the ring and thinks he might get beat, he very likely will. If a tournament fisherman thinks he can't beat the other contestants, he very likely won't.

I've fished with the best fishermen in the world as tournament partners and as competitors. I've always believed I could beat every one of them. I did, more often than not, during my seventeen years of fishing professional bass tournaments.

It cost me money to fish the tournament circuit, as I refused to be sponsored. I absorbed all of my own expenses. I did not want a sponsor telling me what lures to use or what boat to use or what other equipment to use. I didn't want him telling me where to fish a lake at a certain time for the opportunity of being photographed while using his product.

I earned money in the tournaments, of course, in that my name became more and more popular, and therefore so did my lures. People came to know me as the guy who was winning national fishing tournaments by using lures that he made himself. People didn't wonder if my lures worked. They knew by reading the newspaper stories and magazine articles that accompanied each of the tournaments.

I'd eventually grace the covers of *Sports Afield, Outdoor Life,* and *Bass Masters* in one year, unequaled coverage by those magazines.

I was astonished at the sophistication of tournament fishing. Some of the fishermen used an electronic apparatus called a depth finder or fish locator. It was actually a radar-type device that showed the image of live fish and indicated at what depth they swam.

The idea intrigued me. The notion of "seeing" the fish on a screen lessened the sportsmanship in fishing, no doubt. But tournament fishing wasn't for sport, it was for winning. That was the whole idea. The guy who caught the most pounds of bass during the allotted time won the prize money, and an immeasurable amount of publicity that translated into money if he happened to be in the outdoor industry.

I decided I'd give myself the same advantage the other contestants had and utilize a fish locator—one I'd invent myself.

I decided that the depth finders used by most of the fishermen were rife with deficiencies. For example, a fisherman had to stop his boat or the depth finder would not pick up the fish swimming below. Also, the depth finders showed only the fish that were immediately under a fisherman's boat. What about those that were on the perimeter of his boat?

I had never taken a course in electronics. I had never worked for an electronics company.

But I could read.

I read everything I could find about fishing depth finders and how they worked. I read all I could find about radar and how it detected objects underwater. I read how radar noted objects at sea or in the air.

And then I began to experiment.

I made a fish locator that wouldn't have detected a whale with his dorsal fin against the bottom of my boat. So I made another, and another. I played with the construction of a battery-operated radarlike fish locator that would project swimming fish on a screen. My experimentation went on for months.

I read more, experimented more, and failed more to meet the standards I had set for my new machine.

And then I had it.

Working inside my garage or inside a boat with Steve Fulton, an X-ray technician, I eventually hand-crafted a radar detector that would show the image of more fish at a greater depth, and would do so while the fisherman's boat traveled at a rapid speed.

I had made the machine for my own use. I called the man whose company made the world's leading fish locator. I wanted a minimal fee, or nothing at all, for him to put his company's name on my depth finder. For all practical purposes, I was going to "give" him what I knew would be the world's best depth finder.

He wouldn't even look at my creation, not even after I offered to take it to him and to show him personally how my machine was better than any other.

He was simply uninterested.

And so I patented the Humminbird depth finder. I intentionally misspelled the word so it would not be spelled like the bird's. That made it easier to trademark. I selected Humminbird because I thought it was the fastest bird on earth. It isn't. I should have named it "Mallard" if I wanted the name of the fastest bird.

I had become a nationally known fisherman and lure manufacturer who had capital, and the power to borrow more. I enlisted the help of six venture capitalists who bought twenty thousand shares each for one dollar per share. They'd each eventually sell their holdings for more than one million dollars each.

I set up a shop where I taught people to build the Humminbird fish locator. I had created another mass-production business simply because I saw the deficiencies in an existing product, and thought I could build a better one.

The Humminbird became the number-one depth finder in the world. It outsold and outperformed all the competition.

I have had many conversations with the man who makes the second most popular depth finder. We've laughed many times about how he wouldn't see me back when I wanted to give him my new invention. He told me that he and his engineers wouldn't even look at my product because they thought I was a joke, as I initially operated out of my car. What became the world's best-selling fish locator was first marketed the way I first marketed lures—from the trunk of my car. I could personally make each depth finder for about forty dollars, and sell it for one hundred.

I then put it in chain stores, just as I had once moved my lures to chain stores. I also put it in the Bass Pro catalog. Bass Pro is today the nation's leading catalog for fishing gear, and was started by Johnny Morris, an old friend. Bass Pro sold a lot of Humminbirds.

I'm making short another long story about my long road to success.

indicated, I was beginning to attract the attention of the movers and shakers and needy.

I'm always glad to pass along pointers, and will publish another book in the future about how to catch fish. I continue to give pointers on my national television show, *Tom and Tina Outdoors*, as its cohost is Tina Booker, the nation's first female to fill the cohost's role on a national freshwater fishing show. More about her later.

Former Alabama Speaker of the House, the late Jimmy Clark, called in 1967 when he became one of the first public figures to seek my advice about how to land the big ones.

He and I went fishing on Lake Eufaula, the nation's number-one bass lake, which was built by the Corps of Engineers in 1962. The lake was made by controlling the flow of numerous creeks and rivers. It became a 46,000-acre 75-mile-long mecca for fish.

I never tire of bragging about the wonderful lake by my city.

The corps flooded land where giant trees had towered for centuries. Many of those treetops lay just beneath the surface of the water. Herding a boat across the lake, especially in darkness, was tricky.

Clark and I weren't thinking about that after a successful day on the water. We were headed toward dry land as Clark rode in the front of my boat with each of his hands inside his pockets. I was about to mention that his restrained hands would make it impossible for him to brace should the boat stop abruptly. I didn't have time to give him a warning.

The boat ran aground. In the darkness, I had hit a sandbar and the sudden stop hurled Clark out of the boat and into the darkness. He landed on the sandbar but thought he

# CHAPTER NINE

ONE OF THE results of my growing reputation as cessful lure designer and bass fisherman was that celeb business leaders, politicians, and other public figures w to fish with me.

I'd eventually fish with former presidents such as Ji Carter and George Bush, and entertainers such as Dolly ton, Porter Wagoner, and Barbara Mandrell, and ot whose lives interested me. People have written to say they're terminally ill and want to go fishing with me as t last act on earth. I've taken them fishing too.

My benevolence, and celebrity associations, were no commonplace in 1967 as they'd one day become. But, as I was in the water. It was that dark several miles from any illumination.

He began to furiously try to swim.

He kept hollering that swimming was hard, as the water seemed shallow. It was so dark that he didn't realize for several seconds that he was on dry land. He struggled against the water that wasn't there. He went nowhere, of course.

I suggested that he stop "swimming" and simply stand up.

"Oh," the speaker said.

He rose to his feet to feel the side of my boat, stranded high and dry. I drove a specially made Ranger Boat at that time. The manufacturer put two hulls in the boat because I was forever hitting obstructions in the foliage-rich lake. The boat's double construction made it especially heavy.

The speaker and I were perhaps five miles from our dock, the sun was well beneath the horizon, and he posed a lot of questions such as "Did you hear that?" and "Do alligators make sounds when they move on land at night?"

I suggested that we get my boat back into the water. Then I suggested it again. Mr. Clark was transfixed with the sounds of nature that he could hear but not see in the ebony around him.

We couldn't make my boat budge. It was lodged in the sand.

I suggested that we use a stick as a vertical jack—that we shove it in the sand against the bottom of the boat and push the stick forward. That would move the boat.

We felt our way all over the sandbar where we heard wildlife hurry out of our path. We feared the specimen, any specimen, that might not move.

The speaker again asked about the nocturnal sounds of alligators.

I found what I believe was the only stick on the island. I estimate that our boat was fifty feet from the water's edge. We used that branch as a vertical lever, and moved the boat approximately one inch each time we thrust the stick forward. We gained about one foot for every twelve thrusts, and repeated that process fifty times.

It was an exhausting undertaking.

Mr. Clark had many other questions for me about fishing after that ordeal. He posed most of them over the telephone.

THE LATE "Big Jim" Folsom, the former governor of Alabama, initially called me shortly after I became a game warden. He wanted me to check out someone who wanted to contribute to his proposed conservation program. I recommended that he not accept the man's contribution, and he didn't. Folsom and I continued to stay in touch. He had been a two-term governor who liked to fish.

He sought my advice about bass, even though his professional problems overshadowed his personal life. I endorsed his candidacy, but he was not without controversy. I sometimes wondered about the wisdom of our affiliation. Yet, in many ways, I learned some things from him, as he served eight years as the state's chief executive despite his spotted past.

Folsom sent advance men into an area to find out the tastes of the local electorate. When he spoke there, he always endorsed whatever the voters believed in, not always within reason. Most Alabama people wanted nothing more than honesty from politicians.

Folsom ran successfully by using the platform of direct honesty during each of his campaigns. Very direct honesty. They say the truth can hurt. I don't know if my association with Folsom and his openness hurt or surprised me. But as I've indicated, it educated me about not trying to deceive the public.

The controversial Folsom would have actually won a third term had it not been for a single incident: While on television, he got drunk and forgot the names of his children.

I used to follow him through parts of the state, just as he followed me and my advice in a bass boat. Folsom liked to point me out to others in his campaign audiences and tell them I was a self-made man, just like him. In most ways, I was nothing like him.

I remember one speech where he told the people that he was accused of stealing shortly after he assumed office as governor.

"You're damn right I stole," he thundered from the top of an overturned mop bucket that enabled him to stand about a foot taller than those around him. "I stole before those crooks at the capital got it. Old Jim is just telling you the truth!"

The people actually clapped their hands and whistled. The handsome man was loud, charming, and was politics's answer to the circus world of P. T. Barnum. He filled the stereotype that southern politicians would like to forget.

"I'll tell you what," Folsom continued. "The old boys in Montgomery set a trap for me. They baited it with whiskey and women. Let me tell you something, folks. When they bait a trap for old 'Big Jim' with whiskey and women, they'll catch him every time."

I had always been honest, I thought, but this . . .

I also began to receive an increased volume of mail by the end of the 1960s. I answered every letter personally, as I do to this day. Today, of course, most of the correspondence comes as e-mail. I receive about one hundred daily. Each e-mail draws a response, and no response is returned without my first reading it. I try to write as many e-mails personally as possible.

I once received a handwritten, conventional letter that was fourteen pages long. I handed it to my secretary and asked her to tell me what it said in Indian language—meaning for her to give me a two-sentence digest.

"The writer wants some free lures," she replied.

"If he took that much time and that much space to ask, send him some," I said. And she did.

I send each child who writes me a free lure and a catalog. I do that for two reasons. The first is that I feel good whenever I do something for a child. The second is that doing something for a youngster makes a customer for life.

I learned in the late 1960s about the oldest hoax played on celebrity fishermen or lure designers. They receive several letters each year from people who claimed they've endured a garage fire that destroyed all of their fishing tackle. They want free lures as replacements.

I used to send them. Someone once checked out an alleged fire with the letter writer's local fire department. It seems that there was no fire at the writer's house, just a lot of hot air. I thought the request was rude, to put it mildly, and told the author. Shortly afterward, I received another letter from another alleged garage fire victim.

I wondered about the national epidemic of garage arson.

A check, however, also revealed no fire at that address. After it happened a dozen times, I stopped sending lures to people who claimed to have survived garage fires. I did instead send them the names and addresses of competing lure companies, and pointed out that the companies give their slightly defective lures to garage fire victims.

The price of popularity began to carry another price for me in the late 1960s. It's an annoying fee that I pay to this day.

Other lure designers began to counterfeit my lures overseas, especially in China, where American patent laws have no jurisdiction. The lures were beautiful and identical. But they didn't "swim" or run accurately through the water.

I could tell the designers of "knockoffs" exactly what they're doing wrong when they try to imitate my lures. I could—but I won't, as I don't want them to improve their products.

Foreign-made lures usually bear the name of the country in which they were manufactured. All of my lures are manufactured in the United States.

Other lure designers, especially amateurs, began to send me their creations. They wanted me to give them free advice so that they could sell their wares for a fee. I had never asked anyone for advice about anything I had made. But I thought that perhaps I had been blessed with imagination or creativity, and thought that I could give something back to the one who blessed me by helping others. So if someone asked me how he could improve his intended lure, I tried to give him an answer.

Sometimes my response was as direct as "Big Jim" Folsom's might have been.

"A lure that is supposed to 'swim' should not sink immediately to the bottom of the lake, where it instantly becomes hung after being cast," I have written to "designers."

Many lures, then and now, are made by bonding two pieces of plastic. Obviously, the bond should be watertight. To this day, people send me lures that they claim won't "swim." The box in which their lure is packaged and its interior is saturated with water. I have picked up lures that were so filled with water that the bait seemed to pee on me.

"Be sure you make a lure that stays dry inside," I write to such "designers."

The core pin is the most critical part of a lure. That's the pin through which a fisherman's line is tied. The lure's "action," or movement in the water, depends on the core pin's placement.

I can usually look at any lure in progress and tell you with ninety-nine percent accuracy where the core pin should go. Most lure designers implement the skills of engineers with micrometers and the like before making that decision.

Many who don't should.

I remember the first time a man sent me a lure with a letter saying he had created a bait that would become the world's most popular, but that the lure seemed to "tumble" when retrieved through the water. A core pin is usually at the front or sometimes on top of a lure. This particular lure "designer," who couldn't prevent his creation from turning somersaults, had put the core pin on the underside of the bait's tail. Of course the lure spun tail over head in the water.

I didn't know if the guy was chasing fish or gymnasts.

I've been sent lures with core pins misplaced in the tail, eyes, fins, and gills ever since.

A core pin has to be in the center of the lure's vertical side. People have sent me "lures" with the strategic pin situated on one side of the bait's belly.

"It won't swim straight," they have complained.

"It won't swim at all," I have responded.

I asked one guy if he was trying to make lures that appeal to fish who couldn't see. He didn't appreciate my humor.

The word got out that Tom Mann would give free advice on how to design lures. I sometimes wish it hadn't. To this day, I've cast every "lure" that has been sent to me, and evaluated and returned it to its creator with a written critique. It has been a time-consuming and exhaustive task. But it has afforded me that silent joy that comes from trying to help someone else.

This may sound a little strange, but I really don't see lure designing as a job or career. I almost see it as the putting forth of a natural ability, similar to the way I think like a fish. I naturally think about what would appeal to fish, draw and design it, and watch the resulting lure work. Sometimes I change the original design, sometimes I don't. Through trial and error, and through experimentation with fish, I simply "know" when the lure's design is finished—when I can improve it no more. I don't premeditate a lot of my designs, they just "come" to my mind. Sometimes, as I draw them, I feel as though I'm merely holding the pen.

The inspiration comes from beyond me.

# CHAPTER TEN

THE LETTERS OF challenge and dare increased after my mountain of publicity and burgeoning success in 1967. People said I had more than proven myself with freshwater fish.

Now they wanted to see what I could do against that most formidable of underwater opponents—a shark, specifically a great white.

A great white can rip a net of logging rope to shreds. The public wanted to see me take one on a rod and reel.

A lot of fishermen, amateur and professional, had taken sharks with a rod and reel. Few had taken a great white, but it had been done. So what could I do that would be different? Dramatically different.

Then it hit me as hard as a shark would eventually hit my bait: I'd become the first person to take a great white on a rod and reel while fishing from dry land.

How would I do that?

I pondered the question as a few publications reported my vow to take a great white by using essentially the same methods I used to catch freshwater fish. To catch a great white while fishing from a boat was a feat. To catch him while standing on dry land was not only unprecedented, it was unheard of at the time.

Actually, I suspect that through the ages somebody somewhere has hooked a great white and wrestled it to shore. After all, the great white was in the sea before man was on earth. But such a catch had not been documented in 1967.

The public's challenge, and the record books, were waiting.

I went to Destin, Florida, on the Gulf of Mexico. I couldn't afford Australia, where more great whites are found, because of the distance and the cost of living for what could be weeks while I got a great white to take my hook.

I could cast a hundred-pound test line with an incredibly heavy but durable lure for a limited distance. Trouble was, great whites grow to be more than two thousand pounds.

I'd occasionally seen them as much as a mile out in the Gulf, where the water was as much as a quarter mile deep. Even if I cast my light line as far as I could, I'd still be in about twenty-five feet of water above the slow-sloping bottom in the Gulf off Destin. Great whites occasionally shoot through such a shallow, at lightning speed, in search of something larger than an artificial lure. A shark wasn't likely to hit Tom Mann's little six-inch Glow Jig lure unless he was a young tiger shark or other specimen.

I wanted the great white.

I needed a strategy to get my bait to him when he was far from shore, where he didn't have big bait like amberjack or bonita or human beings. Getting to him would mean getting my lure a lot farther out than I could throw it.

If I somehow got it into the bowels of the deep, I'd still have no assurance he'd hit it.

"If I were a shark, what would ensure my strike?" I wondered for days. The press had made a big deal of the fact that I caught fish only on artificial lures that I made myself. I wanted to do the same thing this time.

"What if the shark won't hit anything I designed, which I have no idea how to get to him anyhow?" I wondered.

Then I had it.

The great white, arguably the dumbest fish in the ocean, is likely too dumb to go for anything as new as one of my creations. I'd give that creature of habit what he was used to getting. I would catch one of the great white's natural bait fish on my artificial lure. I would not land the bait fish, I'd instead let him flee into shark-infested waters. The shark would devour him right down to my lure. Then I'd set the hook.

The pier off Destin stretched for one hundred yards into the Gulf. I walked to its end, while a few hundred people gathered behind me. The water was incredibly clear, and I could see the bottom, perhaps fifty feet beneath me. Soon, a school of bonita rushed toward the pier.

I cast my rod, timing the retrieval of my lure so it would move through the school as it swam past me.

I hooked what looked like a ten-pound bonita on the first cast, a respectable catch.

But it wasn't what people had come to see.

"Bonitas attack lures, not people!" one guy shouted.

"Yeah," yelled others, laughing at me and my ten-pound fish, a minnow compared with what they wanted to see.

"Why don't you land your 'trophy'?" one fellow chided. The ridicule yielded to curiosity as I made no effort to reel in the bonita, instead letting it swim into the open ocean.

A bonita bleeds heavily when hooked. That's why I selected it from among the bait fish sought by sharks. Sharks are magnetically drawn to bleeding. They were likely to hit any bonita. They were certain to hit one that was hemorrhaging.

I had three hundred yards of line unreeling at the end of that hundred-yard pier. My hooked bonita swam straight forward. He'd go almost four hundred yards before I'd have to turn him. Turning a ten-pound bonita with a hundred-pound test would be no problem with a deep sea rod.

I had put two feet of steel leader on my nylon line to prevent a shark from cutting it with his teeth. I took reassurance from that as the bonita continued his sprint into the Gulf. He was underwater and still swimming madly when the shark struck.

He must have shattered the bonita on impact, because the shark was instantly hooked. I'd never see the bonita again, only the lure that was torn from the bait fish to lodge in the jaw of the great white.

Seeing my lure protrude from the jaws of the world's most feared predator was a dream come true. A nightmare preceded the dream.

I threw the drag off my reel the instant the shark hit. It was a reflexive movement, the kind that comes from years of going for big fish. Drag simply means the force a fisherman allows his reel to put on his line. It can be increased or decreased with the turn of a dial.

That day, I chose a giant deep-sea reel almost as big as a small skillet. Its drag was practically wide open, allowing the shark to swim freely toward the protective deep.

At his speed, he'd have no trouble popping my hundred-pound test line when he reached the limit of its length. The dumb shark, however, won't swim directly away from anything for very long. It's a shark's nature to swim in circles.

All living things, I figured, resort to their natural instincts when fighting for their lives.

Sure enough, the shark turned in the water. That let pressure off the line. It put pressure on me in a different way, because the great white headed straight for the pier where I stood.

I don't mean to imply I felt my personal safety was threatened. It wasn't. But the shark was swimming toward me faster than I could reel the slack out of the line. If he abruptly turned and headed back out to sea, he'd tighten the line with a jerk. It would then snap in two.

I made myself a human drag. As the shark ran toward me, I ran away from him. I tried to run as rapidly as he was swimming, reeling with every step.

He had pulled the line against me. My running pulled it against him. That kept out slack.

The people on the pier parted to let me run among them from the end of the pier back to the bank. My line was taut, and the shark was closer to land than he'd been since I hooked him.

Then he again made a long dash for the deep.

The line rolled furiously from the loose drag on my reel. To ease the shark's pull, I ran the length of the pier toward the sea. He was running away from me and I was running after him. He could not get my line loose enough to suddenly tighten it with the kind of snap that would set him free.

Again, people parted as I ran as fast as I could through the crowd.

They were cheering, some for the shark, some for me. The more they yelled, the more they attracted other people. Wonderfully, without being asked, they formed single-file lines along the pier, leaving me a path to run up and down as the shark bolted toward and away from the bank.

I was thirty-four years old and still close to my physical prime. I was muscular and determined. I couldn't expend that much energy for four hours today. I'd collapse. That shark fought with the force of a two-hundred-pound fish. Little did I know that he weighed more than twice that much. Much more.

I had run the pier and retrieved perhaps 150 yards of line countless times on the big reel whose crank was about as hard to turn as the propeller on a two-passenger aircraft.

I had wanted to take this fish while facing every disadvantage, but I was beginning to wish I had afforded myself more useful tools. If I'd used a five-hundred-pound test line and if I'd used a rigid deep-sea pole, I could have manhandled that fish into shore within thirty to forty minutes, I thought. I thought the same thing again as my struggle went into its third hour.

And then he surfaced.

His dorsal fin looked like something out of *Jaws*, the movie that wouldn't be released for nine more years. His tail fin looked like a meat cleaver used to dress an elephant.

Those in the crowd, many of whom had become exhausted from standing in the sun and watching my struggle, came alive at the sight of the fish.

"He's three hundred pounds!" one spectator shouted.

"Three-fifty!" shouted another. It sounded like an auction. I couldn't afford to pay attention.

My fight against the behemoth had been flawless. It had to be when pitting a seventeen-pound test line against a weight I knew was outrageously higher. I couldn't let fatigue lessen my concentration. I was tired, very tired. But so was the shark.

It had been a battle of wits and still was. Now it also became a contest of endurance.

My arms ached. I knew that if I had tried to do this on a boat, I'd have worn a leather brace to fortify my throbbing back, and I'd have used a rod holder to let me rest my hands, wrists, and arms.

I had no back brace or rod holder. I had hung on for dear life, hoping I didn't take the shark's. I simply wanted to take him from the ocean and then put him back. I had shoved the butt of my pole into the waist of my trousers. It was pure competition, just me against the fish.

I leapt from the pier onto the beach. I could sense the fish would not be sprinting back out to sea. He was drained and fading as fast as I was. One of us would lose soon. Getting careless would have been easy.

The line had been stretched to the maximum length time after time. Each time, just in time, I had absorbed its tension with the reel's drag or the drag afforded by my footwork.

I could run no more. The fish was pulling at my rod now. He was nudging it. Yet the mere nudge of a fish that size could render force ten times beyond my line's capacity to hold it.

Then there was the lure that had caught the bonita that had caught the shark. It was not made for monsters with gills. Would it straighten enough to free the fish? The hook could have pulled a truck without straightening. But not for this long.

And so the war continued.

The sun was setting. The fish had gone back down and was still swimming. I was hurting in every place I could feel sensation.

The crowd, even those who had cheered for me, began to walk away.

"He'll never land that thing," I heard one person mutter. I had not quit fighting and neither had the fish. The audience was nonetheless quitting its vigil.

I felt a sense of betrayal for me and for the shark.

I was suddenly, somehow psychologically pulling for the fish that was physically pulling against me. If my line had been big, and if I'd have tightened the reel's drag, the shark would have pulled me into the water. I would have let him before I would have let go of the rod.

I felt a groundswell of determination. I got my second wind for the fiftieth time.

I had reeled the shark closer to shore than he'd been all day. I could see him flounder maybe twenty yards from me.

Then, as if he knew what he was doing, he surrendered. He used what would be his last burst of energy to shoot for land—dry land. The shark's momentum carried him from the water onto the shore and up to my feet. He visibly moved his gills in what appeared to be an exaggerated gesture. Then he moved them no more.

He died in my shadow. I was the last thing he ever saw. In a curious way, the fish had won, as I had wanted to take him alive. He denied that by fighting to his death. It was as if he wanted me to see him die, his only satisfaction from a fight lost forever.

Seven men leapt into the water, some wading to their waists. Two put their hands inside his gills on either side. The remaining five hoisted his body.

When it had become apparent I was actually going to conquer the giant, the crowd returned in even larger numbers than before. I'd guess more than a thousand people saw a solitary fisherman land a great white by ushering it to shore without a gaff or net, just as he would a pan-size catfish. As the fish was lifted from the water, spectators erupted into applause. I immediately recognized that my catch was not a great white after all but a massive tiger shark.

I waved to the crowd. Merely lifting my arm was painful. I hurt, indeed I throbbed, all over for days afterward.

The shark was lifted onto a truck and taken to a giant scale, where a pulley hoisted him in the air by his tail. The weight meter stopped firmly at 503 pounds. Onlookers exploded into applause the way they do when a golfer wins a major PGA tournament by a single stroke on a final putt.

Pictures, of course, were taken of the shark and me.

I don't have one. Not one. I choose to remember my foe as the fighter he was while alive. I don't want to see photographs of his dormant torso, devoid of life and dripping with blood. He had been a magnificent creature who deserved dignity in death, as he'd had it in life.

I did what many thought couldn't be done and what I, at times, thought I couldn't do. Somehow, I felt as much remorse as pride.

The catch brought my lure companies a million dollars worth of publicity and patronage. In 1967, a million dollars was a lot of money.

To this day, I wouldn't take a million dollars for the experience, but I wouldn't give a penny to do it again.

# CHAPTER ELEVEN

I CONTINUED TO fish tournaments and to sell lures through the end of the 1960s and into the 1970s, when I caught one fish that to the average viewer was an average fish.

I took one look at the fish and felt as if I'd known him personally all my life. It was apparent to me that he had personality. That little bass, more than the hundreds of thousands of others that I've caught, changed my life forever.

My studying his behavior, especially his eating habits, taught me more about how to think like a fish than anyone or anything else. Until I befriended that fish, I thought I could only think like a fish.

As recently as August 2001, that fish was still getting national coverage, as *Southern Living* magazine did a feature article about him twenty years after his death, twenty-eight after I caught him.

The following story, if you don't know it, will sound like the fish story of all fish stories. But it has been documented by numerous outdoor and feature magazines as well as the Associated Press, United Press International, and other news-gathering organizations.

Some of the mass media made small errors in their coverage. That much ink about a solitary fish is bound to carry some mistakes. So let me set the record straight about a fish that my wife named Leroy Brown.

I caught the one-pound largemouth, a fish slightly larger than the average largemouth, on one of my lures. As I reached to take him off the hook, I noticed his eyes. They seemed to be closer together than other largemouth's. They were more on the top of his head and less on the side. And they actually seemed to focus.

I looked at the fish and could tell he was looking back at me. He spoke with his stare.

I carried him home and put him in my swimming pool, where I once kept giant fish. Leroy was smaller than any other fish in the pool.

I used the fish to learn how to catch fish. I used to experiment with lures and retrieving in that pool behind my house.

Leroy never again hit a lure with a hook. I had caught him on a hook, and that was the last time I'd ever trick him. I don't fish for bass with live bait, as that would be a negative endorsement for an artificial lure designer. But I occasionally threw live bait to Leroy when he was in captivity.

He would strike and devour it, but not if it contained a hook, no matter where it was concealed. I studied the way he ate when he chose to, noticing how much water a bass "inhales" as he swallows. My subsequent studies revealed that it's approximately one gallon. I noticed the way Leroy would carry a lure before deciding whether he wanted to ingest it, and then I began to notice that practice among other bass in the aquarium.

Leroy taught me more than they because he was daring. He'd do whatever he wanted to do in full view of me, while other bass would remain hidden behind structure that I had situated in the environment I'd created for them.

Before long, Leroy was accompanied by three large female bass inside my pool. Sometimes, when one of the females shot for one of my experimental lures, Leroy darted into her path, defraying her strike. He protected his women. Leroy had a swimming and happy harem.

I never caught one of his girlfriends on one of my lures, no matter how much they tried to get to it. Leroy always thwarted their efforts.

Leroy was the Jimmy Cagney of fish—little, tough, worldly wise, and a lady-killer. Some of his female fish were six times his weight. They were nonetheless spellbound by Leroy, then only eight inches from tail to lip.

I took Leroy out of my pool and put him inside a 38,000-gallon aquarium that I still maintain at Tom Mann's Fish World, my tourist attraction in Eufaula. The aquarium was filled with larger fish, and was built with the idea of studying fish and filming lure commercials through its glass walls.

I wanted to see just how much of a survivor Leroy really was. He had chased large fish out of one end of my swimming pool, maintaining half of the pool for him or his girlfriends, whom he saw as guests. I wondered if he'd be as dominant among the twenty-pound catfish that floated through my aquarium.

I didn't want Leroy to get hurt. But he was certainly no prize bass to the average customer who paid to walk through the aquarium with its giant and looming game and predatory fish.

Leroy hit the aquarium water, swam directly to the biggest catfish in the tank, and slapped the fire out of him with his tail.

I've never seen anything like that from that day until this.

He sought his enemy and then he beat him. And then he darted as fast as he could into the side of the next catfish and then the next. Then he started on the larger largemouths, and he whipped every one of them too.

In a matter of minutes, Leroy was the lord and master of an aquarium that is perhaps ten percent as long as a city block!

I couldn't believe what I was seeing. Leroy was a tiny freshwater bass, not a ferocious saltwater shark. I wondered if he knew that.

Whenever he beat the spirit out of a larger fish, which, as I've indicated, was all the other fish in the aquarium, he'd swim past me as they swam madly for cover. It was as if he knew what he was doing and wanted to brag before me. I think Leroy would have winked at me if he'd had eyelids.

And then, from the deepest spot of the pool, rose my one

and only bullfin, a prehistoric fish found throughout the South. Bullfin ran on land like lizards millions of years ago. They have sharp teeth like a northern pike. They eat smaller fish, larger fish, and just about anything else that swims.

I had been fascinated by Leroy. I hated to see him go. But who was I to interfere in nature's survival of the fittest, or so I thought in 1973.

The big bullfin cast a shadow across Leroy as he floated toward the smaller fish. The bullfin was in no hurry to swim to the competition, as his killer instincts told him there wouldn't be any. There wasn't. Leroy charged the monster.

With no teeth, Leroy locked mouths with the giant. The two fish rolled end over end in the water. Leroy was firmly in the grips of the bullfin, and blood began to float into the aquarium.

I suddenly wished that Leroy wasn't even in the water. I wanted my unusual fish out of harm's way thrown by the ugly giant. In a short time, he was.

Each time the bullfin opened his mouth to swallow Leroy, Leroy swam farther into the big fish's throat. I think that Leroy was thinking he'd choke the large aggressor.

It didn't happen. The blood flowed and the water boiled. And then the bullfin, arguably the most aggressive freshwater fish in North America, jerked madly from the clasp of little Leroy. He did not get completely away, however, without Leroy's swatting the big fish with the breadth of his tiny tail.

If the swat had happened above instead of beneath water, I think it could have been heard.

The little fish that had won control of half of my swimming pool now had one half of my aquarium, eighteen thousand gallons of water, all to himself. During the next eight years, not one fish ever went into Leroy's side of the aquarium, unless it was one of his girlfriends. When Leroy was "done" with a girlfriend, he'd forcefully charge her in the side, running her back to the other fish at the opposite end of the tank. He didn't see her again until he felt the urge.

My fish was a chauvinist pig.

Then he swam or held motionlessly alone in *his* end of the tank, while about twenty other fish and turtles fought for space in theirs.

Neither I nor the legions of sportswriters and fishing enthusiasts who saw Leroy had ever seen anything like him.

The little fish, his independence and savvy, began to get more publicity than I did. I was fishing national bass tournaments and making millions of dollars in a lure business that had sprung from a cottage industry. But a set of gills that wouldn't have measured two inches was getting miles and miles of newspaper space.

Many of the stories and articles are on display in my museum today.

Back in the early 1970s, I wondered how a little fish could prove to be more competitive as a public figure than the nation's top bass fisherman. Something was wrong with that picture.

Speaking of pictures, Leroy was camera happy.

If we tried to shoot a television commercial for one of my lures, and tried to prove that it would attract big bass, Leroy would swim into the camera's view, upstaging the trophy fish. I didn't want him in the shot. People didn't want to buy lures that attracted small fish like Leroy.

I'd sometimes have to use a net to take Leroy out of the

aquarium completely before I could shoot a commercial. The other fish would invade Leroy's territory as soon as he was out of it. They'd hurry to their own as soon as he was returned to it.

Was this little guy a bass or a bouncer? Just how smart was he?

I decided I'd try to train him.

He obviously had aptitude. Everyone in my immediate circles said I should leave well enough alone. I'd gotten a lot of valuable publicity due to Leroy's independent and fighting triumphs.

Perhaps I should not try to tap his intelligence, I was advised. If I failed, the public would think that Leroy's incredible accomplishments had reached their peak.

"Fish don't think," people said.

I had known better before I met Leroy. His behavior had confirmed it to me. I wanted to teach something to Leroy. Leroy wanted to learn from me.

I could sense it.

By that time, more and more youngsters were coming into my exhibit and asking, "Where is Leroy Brown?" That question was posed much more than "Where is Tom Mann?"

I decided to train Leroy to eat minnows from my hand.

I began by throwing them into the air and letting him strike them as they hit the water. Suddenly, while a minnow was in midair, Leroy leapt from the water and clobbered it. He did it again and again. Each time, the minnow would be a bit closer to my hand when he bopped it. I threw live bait as opposed to artificial because I wasn't trying to catch Leroy.

Then I held a minnow over the aquarium and he bolted

skyward like a trained porpoise. Bam! Leroy took it from my hand.

Word of mouth had spread across Eufaula that I was going to try to train a bass. That attracted an increasing number of local admirers. When Leroy jerked the first minnow from between my thumb and index finger, a rise of applause filled the hollow air above the bubbling aquarium.

I'm starting to disbelieve some of this story myself. But it's nonetheless true. I've read it; I've lived it.

I eventually held a hula hoop above the water for Leroy. You got it. A wild bass, whose brothers and sisters live only for the impulse to eat, charged from the water and sailed through the air, penetrating the center of the hula hoop. Astonishing, and probably unprecedented, for a freshwater species.

That airborne stunt became an act for Leroy. After he'd done it once, he did it whenever I held the hoop above the water.

I took delight in the fact that he'd do it only for me.

But the little bass that was making me more famous was also making me look a bit foolish. Here I was, the nation's top designer of artificial lures, and I couldn't make one that would trick one little fish. Actually, he wasn't so little, as he had grown to perhaps two or three pounds by then.

The popularity of plastic worms was continuing to accelerate in the bass lure industry. Whenever one throws a plastic worm, he buries the hook inside the worm, making the hook invisible and the lure weedless.

Leroy could be tricked by what he couldn't see, I decided. He'd hit one of my famous worms, especially the Jelly

Worm, the most popular fishing worm in the world, I was sure.

I strategically hid the hook's point in the Jelly Worm before dragging my rig across the bottom of the aquarium.

Here came Leroy.

I expected him to charge hard into the worm, as if he were killing it. Then, while it was "stunned," Leroy would devour the worm that he, like all other bass, would think was real.

Leroy charged the Jelly Worm, halted, examined the lure, and shoved his tail under it. He literally shoveled the worm from the bottom of the aquarium. He then took the worm for a ride on his tail, made horizontal as Leroy swam on his side.

That fish was straight out of Ringling Bros. and Barnum & Bailey!

Leroy got applause for not being outsmarted. I got red with embarrassment for myself, with fascination for Leroy.

I threw plastic worms in little pieces at Leroy and he ate them. Whenever I threw one with a highly hidden hook, he took it for a ride on his tail as if he were mocking me.

He was.

I had hooked that fish only once in my life. I could have hooked him again only with a speargun, which I wouldn't have fired, as I had fallen in love with Leroy. So had the nation.

Again, this story is about a bass.

Leroy Brown had put me on the map as much or more than my own fishing and manufacturing feats. I decided I owed him, and that I could pay him in only one way.

I had to set him free.

I drained my aquarium to clean it, and when I was finished, I eased Leroy into a little private pond. I put his aquarium roommates with him. I returned the other fish to the aquarium by dipping them by hand from the water. All were present except Leroy. He was not to be found.

I missed him and I wanted him back. So did the public.

So I seined the pond, but to no avail. My workers and I made repeated passes with our seine. Nothing.

I was dying to get Leroy back into the environment from which I had freed him. I wasn't free without him, and I was sure he felt the same about me.

So I drained the lake. I drained the entire lake to capture one scrawny fish!

I found turtles, carp, bass, snakes, and a baby alligator. I did not find Leroy. He clearly had to be absent.

I thought he'd been smart enough to escape the seine. The fact was, I decided, that Leroy was gone. Perhaps he'd picked on the wrong big fish and had been eaten. Perhaps the alligator had gotten him. Maybe, just maybe, a fisherman more talented than I had sneaked onto the lake and had done what I'd failed do, caught him on a hook. No, I decided, Leroy's absence was not the result of the impossible.

So life minus Leroy began. People continued to come from across the nation by the hundreds to see him. I had one tired answer for them all.

"He's gone," I said. "I put him in the lake near my house and now he's gone. That's all I know."

I grew tired of people asking the same question, and more tired of asking it to myself.

It had taken time for me to bond with Leroy. Now I'd need time to heal from his disappearance. I missed him for about a year during the two weeks he was gone.

I went once more to the lake and was nonchalantly reading the surface of the water for signs of fish, as I do by habit
whenever I look at water. I saw structure, a weed bed, and
thought there might be at least one bass beneath it.

My thought was confirmed when two eyes popped
through the top of the water and stared straight at me as if
they belonged to a turtle. Fish don't stare. But one fish had.
I'd seen that look as it looked through me too many times.

Leroy was alive. He wanted me to know that, and he
wanted me to know that I could live with that knowledge,
but without him.

Needless to say, I tried to get him to hit a lure, but he
wouldn't. Where had he gone when the lake was drained? I
don't know to this day. I wished the little guy could talk, and
had felt long ago that he had the same wish.

My workmen and I went back after Leroy Brown, not
with one seine, but with scores. I anchored them to the
ground and covered the entire weed bed where I had seen
him last. I built a cage of net to catch an elusive, and apparently occasionally invisible, fish.

Then I tightened the walls of the cage. I moved the vertical walls toward the side of the weed bed and lowered the
overhead wall to top of it. Leroy's swimming space had been
reduced to a few square feet.

Once again, the entire pond was drained. All of this for
a fish. I could have caught an entire stringer of larger fish in
a fraction of the time and virtually without effort. But I did
it for a runt who could put himself and, obviously me,
through hoops.

The water was lowered to an amount that was no more

than a pool on the bottom of the pond. Then the pool was reduced as the last drops of water inched from the basin. When the remaining pond was about four inches deep, a dorsal fin protruded.

It belonged to Leroy, the only fish left in the pond. I took no chances. I drained the water until the overhead net fell on Leroy's back. Then I picked him up by hand and the workmen applauded.

I wondered how many times I'd heard people applaud for a fish who couldn't hear clapping. Or could he? I had decided not to underestimate any creature that could determine the reality of an underwater worm just by looking, when many humans could not, and who could jump through hoops and evade more men than an escaped fugitive.

People said I shouldn't be frustrated because Leroy couldn't speak, and suggested that I teach him to write with his fin. This entire Leroy Brown mania was so wonderfully out of hand. And Leroy was back in his aquarium!

Perhaps the return killed him.

Leroy Brown died of old age. Natural causes. Maybe a heart attack. His death just happened to coincide with the opening of a giant BASS tournament on Lake Eufaula. Thousands of fishermen and fans were on hand. I later wondered if he knew that his passing was a publicist's dream.

An obituary about Leroy appeared the next day in the Eufaula newspaper, and it was moved over news wires to newspapers around the world.

I did what I'd do for a human being, and buried Leroy two days after he'd passed. I had no idea that he'd actually be bigger in death than he was in life.

including Hank Parker. The governor of Alabama and a few state legislators were also on hand.

I hoped that Leroy wouldn't offend. He hadn't been embalmed.

The story of this fish has taken on a chronology that puts my own ahead of itself. It is now 1981, and I'll digress to my own chronology at this chapter's end. But for now, I thought you'd want to hear Leroy's story right up until its closing.

In the presence of hundreds of tearful onlookers, I buried Leroy Brown behind Tom Mann's Fish World, by then one of the nation's top retail attractions for fishermen. Mourners laid wreaths, assorted flowers, and plastic worms on top of his grave.

The next day, all the decorations were gone. In their place was a short note. It asked for ten thousand dollars for the return of Leroy's body. Grave robbers had dug it up during the night.

I asked my secretary to buy space in the Eufaula newspaper saying that I'd pay the ransom. Leroy's shrunken scales and withered gills meant that much to me. Besides, I had already spent a small fortune on his casket, the funeral, and a monument. I knew that folks would come, as they did, for years to bawl over the grave of what surely must have been the most intelligent freshwater fish with attitude in history. How would they feel about crying over an empty tomb? I had to recover Leroy for their sake, I rationalized.

One guy said he didn't think Leroy had been stolen at all. He attributed the disappearance to a resurrection.

Do you doubt Leroy mania or its impact on my career and reputation?

number, she said, and added that she wouldn't be surprised if the call was long distance.

It was traced to an airlines baggage claim in Tulsa, Oklahoma.

Susanne called the number and spoke to someone who knew nothing about a call to Tom Mann, and who asked why Mann had held that famous fish's funeral before he could get there.

Susanne thanked him and she hung up. The telephone rang four days later. It was the airlines baggage claim department.

"Describe the casket that Leroy Brown is in," ordered the caller.

Susanne described the casket and coffin in which she'd last seen Leroy.

"Yep," we got him, said the baggage handler. "I know it's him because your description fits the package that stinks to high heaven."

Leroy still had not been embalmed.

The caller declined the finances for fins regarding Leroy. He sent Leroy to Eufaula in a plastic Baggie. He kept the satin-lined tackle box.

Leroy weighed six pounds and two ounces at death, pretty big for a male bass. In all of his traveling, he had deteriorated to perhaps two odorous pounds.

A second and private burial was held behind my tourist attraction.

I spent four thousand dollars to have a monument carved by hand in Germany. To this day, it is the most photographed attraction on the grounds of Tom Mann's Fish World.

My wife, who I've indicated has tried to curb my wild spending, goaded me for having spent four thousand dollars two decades ago for a marble monument to a dead fish.

I settled her by pointing out that the monument was of interest to hundreds of ticket-buying museum attendants, and that if she'd notice, I had inscribed Leroy's name on only one side of the marker.

"The other side of the monument," I told her, "is reserved for you."

# CHAPTER TWELVE

MY 38,000-GALLON AQUARIUM was, for a long time, the largest freshwater fish tank east of the Mississippi River. It's part of the Tom Mann Fish World, my retail complex for which ground was broken in stages during the 1970s, when my popularity on the bass circuit continued to grow.

I went on to build a sporting goods store and a museum that address historic causes with which I'm sympathetic, such as the plight of the American Indian, whose land was stolen from him by the white man in the second half of the nineteenth century. As part Cherokee, I resent the injustice, and I always will.

Tourists came in droves to Fish World, and had no

hesitation about telling me what they wanted and didn't want to see inside my facility. Many, for example, wanted to marvel at the giant fish that I've caught. Some fish swim in the aquarium, others are mounted on its walls. I also have about fifty of my tournament trophies displayed.

I even mounted those fish taken on Lake Eufaula, where a buddy and I caught more pounds of bass than have ever been taken during one day by two men with a rod and reel. I included a mounted replica of the world's largest largemouth, that fish caught in Georgia in 1932 by George Perry. The fish weighed twenty-two pounds four ounces. The Depression farmer who caught it needed it for nutrition, and he and his children ate it.

Tom Mann's Fish World also eventually offered for sale every fishing lure I ever designed, as well as the Humminbird Depth Finder. They're sold with other fishing gear.

The Mann Bait Co., Tom Mann Lures, Inc., Techsonic Industries (makers of the Humminbird), Southern Plastics (a plastic worm company I'd open in a few years), and my Fish World would collectively become Eufaula's largest employer. Long before that happened, my economically modest years would be old news, and my family and I came to know an annual income solidly into seven figures. I asked my wife if she was proud of what we'd done, after having chased our dream from our kitchen through the long corridors of commerce. I posed the question after randomly handing her a check for one million dollars.

"I'm proud of your success," she said. "But I was most proud the first time I was able to get through the grocery store checkout line without having to take something back to the shelf."

All of my entities are built around the bass.

Ray Scott, whose BASS tournaments were solidly off and running, had no idea in the middle 1970s that BASS would one day promote the annual Grand Masters Tournament to decide the national bass fishing championship on network television. Earlier, neither he nor I, while waiting in long gasoline lines during the oil embargo, had a clue that freshwater fishing would one day be practiced weekly by forty million Americans, according to a 2000 story in *USA Today,* or that it would become a $108-billion annual industry by 2001, according to a front-page story in *The Wall Street Journal.*

Nothing has done more to promote bass fishing than BASS, which today claims four times as many members as the Professional Golfers Association. No one did more to promote BASS during its formative years than its charter members.

Scott, like a lot of successful men, is sometimes impatient. That was clear as he struggled to make BASS an expanding outfit. He wanted the organization to become a household word, which it already was among bass fishermen. He wanted it to also become familiar to nonfishermen as well.

Ray insisted that those of us who regularly fished the bass tournaments, covered by the national outdoor magazines, take his organization and ourselves to the people. He asked a few tournament fishermen to leave their bass boats, to depart their own businesses, and go on a tour of one-night speaking engagements for two weeks out of every month. He said the public needed to see the flesh and blood behind our names.

I thought Ray was asking a lot. Our businesses were paying us more than he could pay us for public speaking, just as they paid us more than he could pay us for fishing his bass tournaments. But the tournaments had proven to be invaluable as promotional vehicles for our products, especially my fishing lures. Ray assured us that after we endeared ourselves to the American people, we'd see still more interest in our respective enterprises.

So, with my heart in my throat and my hope up in arms, I went on the 1976 BASS Blue Bird bus tour, my first encounter with public speaking.

Roland Martin, the bass fishing genius from South Carolina, was also on that first tour, along with legendary fisherman Bill Dance as well as Stan Sloner. Harold Sharp was our front man, and Ray stood in the background, where he did what he does best. He collected the public's money.

We were a mobile package show, a group presentation about fishing. And we were a hit.

We played every state in the nation except Montana, doing several one-nighters in several cities in some states. I spent a million monotonous miles on the Blue Bird bus.

We rode inside a customized bus like those used by touring entertainers. It had a refrigerator, a microwave oven, a dining area, and other accessories that made our place an apartment on twelve wheels. Bus travel gave a sense of dislocation like I haven't had to this day. We'd go to sleep, while sitting up, in one city and wake up in another five hundred miles away. We'd present a show and get a motel, unless the next town on the tour required that we depart that very night. Before long, all of the venues and motel rooms began to look the same. Soon, the days were the same, as each had essentially the same routine.

I'd heard about entertainers who travel so much they don't know what day of the week it is, or in what city they're located. That happened to me. It didn't matter what day it was. The show had to go on, then the cast had to go to the next town.

It was fourteen days of that, then fourteen days as a suburban dweller before going back to the bus and the road.

I was living my life in a marathon that wouldn't stop. I'd been asked to get on board. I was soon, at times, asking myself how to get off.

I had no idea that there were so many cultural differences inside our nation. The fishermen in Texas and California, for example, were very knowledgeable and in tune with the spirit of recreational or competitive bass fishing. We speakers essentially told fishing stories. They laughed harder at the funny ones, and gasped more at the dramatic ones, than the fishermen in other parts of the nation.

We went to places where there was virtually no audience response. We thought we were "bombing" before the tiny gatherings. Then our presentation was often followed by a block-long line of quiet fans who bought all of the wares we had for sale.

I remember I sold a manual about fishing. It was pocket size and went for $4.95. The manual receipts, as well as my share of the gate, sometimes paid me thousands of dollars a day. That wasn't a bad day's pay in 1976, year of the nation's two hundredth anniversary.

We played Omaha, Nebraska, and drew seven thousand

bass fishermen. That might not be an enormous crowd by today's standards. But it was tremendous in 1976, when no BASS tournament or tournament fisherman had yet drawn national broadcast exposure. We were just a bunch of anglers who'd been amateurs a few years earlier.

Our very first date was in Columbus, Georgia, a city about ninety minutes from Eufaula. I'd heard entertainers say that your hometown is always the hardest venue to play. Columbus was an extension of my hometown. I thought it was unfortunate that my first engagement should be touted as my hardest.

The touting was accurate.

Ray himself introduced me, and he went on and on, bragging about me during my introduction. It was embarrassing.

I was so impressed with what he was saying that I could hardly wait to hear what I had to say.

I was supposed to do thirty minutes in what I fondly remember as my "popcorn speech." I leapt up, turned white, and sat down.

Before I did, however, I mumbled a few stories about my fishing experiences on the tournament trail, and as a lad.

I had been talked into this job. Suddenly, as my voice echoed through the hall where an occasional member of the audience yawned or scratched, I felt misplaced.

Why on earth would any of these people care about the fishing tales of a man they've never met? I wondered to myself.

I recited some of my more unusual experiences, however, and they went "oooh." I told a humorous story or two and they belly-laughed. I mentioned I'd made notes that I'd put into a published booklet that was for sale in the lobby, and some of them jumped up to get in line before I ever quit speaking.

That experience, a quarter-century ago, was my most vivid lesson to date about the fascination that some people hold for someone who can think like a fish enough to make a lure that a fish finds appetizing. The people's fascination was compounded because I could sink my lure and catch a hidden bass that my instincts told me was there.

I previously had no idea that so many people thought that those of us on the tour, a bunch of backwoods fishermen, were special. I was accustomed to sweating while making lures or throwing them at fish. In those undertakings, I didn't feel special. Onstage, it was different.

I was out of the sunlight and in a spotlight. My every sentence was sometimes followed by applause, as if I were a politician promising prosperity. When I left the platform, people wanted to be photographed with me. They wanted my autograph, and they wanted additional autographs for relatives and friends.

All of that for an ole boy raised a few miles from Penton, Alabama? All of that attention just because I knew how to catch fish? Yes.

I couldn't decide if I liked being a celebrity. Fishing is a solitary sport often performed out of an onlooker's sight. Suddenly, my photograph was appearing in the next day's newspapers in towns where I'd simply opened my mouth, something I'd made my living encouraging fish to do.

It was confusing. At times, it was fun.

And it was stressful. I liked to catch fish. I didn't like living in a fishbowl.

The idea of having some reporter "review" my words, spoken through free association, was overwhelming. Why did the reporters write what I wore and what got a laugh? Did anyone really care?

I think the other fishermen on that first tour felt the same way—totally disarmed by the press and public attention that we'd eventually take for granted. We knew the pressure of tournament competition, not of celebrity status. The latter pressure didn't stop after four days of competition. It expanded until it was vented.

And so we learned to vent. Men whose remarks were recorded as public record at night became boys whose mischief was sometimes public nuisance later at night.

We played a date in Florida, for example, where heavy tourism reinforced the nation's gasoline shortage. Motels were full. Vacationers remained in lodging rather than driving to various attractions, fearful they'd run out of gasoline.

Harold told an innkeeper that he thought we should receive a reduced room rate, as we had arrived in the middle of the night and would be guests for only a few hours. The desk clerk told Harold to pay the outrageously high rate or return to the bus.

"We've got so much business that we don't need yours," he told Harold.

People didn't talk to other people in that tone in Penton.

We were tired and bored with the bus. We didn't want to face another mile. Moreover, we didn't want to hear the guff of a proprietor who, in theory, was supposed to be polite to the public.

"I don't give a damn whether a bunch of hillbilly fishermen stay at this motel or not," he added.

That was it. The next fish we caught would be behind the registration desk.

We paid the outrageous room rate and began the task of dragging our bags to our beds at three A.M. Ray was still doing a slow burn over the innkeeper's prices and attitude.

He discovered that Bill and Stan were sharing a room. Despite the high rate, we had to sleep two to a room. Ray told Bill and Stan he'd help them with their bags, and asked one for his room key.

He went to their room, didn't take a single bag, and crawled under the covers in one of the beds. He would use Bill and Stan as guinea pigs to make the desk clerk a victim.

When Bill and Stan sleepily stumbled into their room, Ray bolted upright in bed. He screamed in a high voice, as if he were a woman. In the darkness, they couldn't see.

The two frightened fishermen shot for the front desk.

"What do you mean charging these goofy rates for a room that's occupied?" one said. "We just scared some old gal to death. There could be a lawsuit. Now give us a room that's vacant."

"I can't," replied the desk clerk. "I sold our last room since you guys checked in."

"What?" Bill said. "That was just a few minutes ago."

"Business is good," the clerk said, grinning.

Bill and Stan weren't amused. They demanded that the desk clerk come with them to their assigned room and evict the woman who was sleeping in one of their beds.

Ray, in the meantime, had gotten out of the bed, and had put the bedspread neatly back in place. When the proprietor used a pass key to open the door, the room was neat—and vacant.

"What is it with you guys?" the desk clerk shouted. "Just how far *have* you traveled? Are you hallucinating? No one is in this room. I suggest you take it."

An interior door separated the room in question from the adjacent room, where Ray muffled his laughter. He heard the innkeeper stomp away, and he heard Bill and Stan let the door close as they gathered the luggage they had scattered in the hall while fleeing a "woman's" screams. Ray instantly shot through the interior door back into their room. Again, he covered himself in the bed.

Again, Bill and Stan tried to wearily wrestle their bags through the door and into the dark room. Again, Ray didn't give either time to find the light switch.

He sat up in bed more forcefully than the last time.

"Rape! Rape!" he screamed in his falsetto.

One of the fishermen stopped grabbing for the light switch and put both hands protectively over his pelvis, I was later told.

The two sprinted for the front desk. Their lack of amusement had transformed into a presence of fury.

"Listen you little son of a bitch!" one of them later claimed he said. "You done rented us a room with a woman who's hollering rape. The law could be coming through the door any minute. Let's hope he don't come to investigate your murder. Now, get us a damn room without nobody in it!"

The desk clerk was terrified, I later heard. But what could he do? He couldn't give them what he didn't have. So he insisted that this time he'd walk back to the room in question, and that he'd go inside.

By then Ray had once again fluffed the pillows and

made the bed. He returned to his own room, leaving no sign of entrance.

From his hideout, he heard the innkeeper burst into the first room while hollering, "Who's in here, who's in here?"

Silence. Ray heard the trio walk around the bed, and heard one of them say, "She ain't under the bed."

"Now, listen," said the desk clerk. "I know you guys are unhappy about the rates, but either take this *empty* room or go on down the highway."

One of the fishermen accused him of trying to run them off so he could rent out the room a second time in one night.

The man said he was insulted. The fisherman urged him to be glad he was conscious.

At least two other guests had poured into the hall to investigate the disturbance. One was a woman with cream smeared all over her face and giant curlers in her hair. One fisherman asked her if there was additional life on Mars.

Tired men have short fuses and quick wits.

The innkeeper went back to his desk, Ray sprinted back to Bill and Stan's bed, and a "woman" eventually sat upright in bed—for the third time.

"Help! Help!" she screamed. "I'm being attacked by two ugly men!"

Bill and Stan darted again for the innkeeper. He threatened to call the police, and Stan reportedly offered to dial the telephone. Somebody mentioned having the desk clerk arrested for fraud—renting a room to two men after first renting it to one woman.

Of course there was a search and of course no trespasser was found. One of the fishermen angrily threatened to knock on every door in the motel to find the hysterical woman.

"I'll wake up this whole damn place!" he said.

The desk clerk asked the men to quietly retire. He said he'd stand outside their door until they yelled that they were in bed. And, he said, if they'd lie down quietly, their room fee would be returned.

That's what Ray had wanted.

Madness gave way to fatigue. The fishermen went to sleep, perhaps dreaming about the high lodging fee that they wouldn't have to pay.

The misbehaved Ray had literally gotten the room fees reduced to nothing. But someone in the group who shall remain nameless wasn't happy. He thought that free lodging only made us even with the rude innkeeper. It would take free lodging for other guests, he thought, to put us ahead.

A golf course was next to the motel, where guests could open their patio doors and watch the duffers as they hit their ball onto a fairway. One of the fishermen went to a room, knocked on the door, and introduced himself as the professional sportsman he was. He said that he had an interest in golf, and wondered if it would be all right for him to come inside to watch the golfers as they hit their first shot on the outside hole.

The motel guest received him, and wanted to talk about fishing and what it was like to earn a living doing it. The fisherman was nice to the guest.

"Let's open your patio door," he said to the guest. "We can see the golfers clearly as they approach the fairway."

That was fine with the guest, obviously flattered to have a professional fisherman in his room.

Soon, the first golfer approached the fairway. He put his tee in the ground and composed himself over the ball for a long drive.

"Let's stand up," the fisherman said to his host. "We can see better."

The motel guest walked to the patio, opened the door, and watched the golfer as he began his back swing. As the golfer swung forward, the fisherman yelled loudly.

"This motel has bugs!"

The golfer threw his club, missing the ball entirely.

He looked up to glare at the motel guest who had received the fisherman. The fisherman, by then, had shot out the other door, into the hall, and out of sight.

The golfer angrily approached the motel guest.

"What do you mean yelling when I was trying to swing?" he thundered. "You cost me a stroke!"

"I didn't yell," insisted the motel guest.

"Oh, yeah?" said the golfer. "Then who did, a ghost?"

"No, a fisherman."

He should have said it was a ghost. He would have been more believable.

"A fisherman?" yelled the golfer. "Where was he fishing, in your bathtub?"

The fisherman by then had knocked on another motel door and had put the same spiel on another guest, identifying himself and suggesting that the guest, his wife, and the fisherman watch a golfer as he approached the hole.

The beleaguered innkeeper, by then, was looking for the golfer, who'd checked out earlier but was apparently still on the premises.

A new golfer came to the same hole and the fisherman

again tricked the guest into standing in front of him. The fisherman again yelled as the golfer swung, and the golfer drove his driver into the dirt.

He was also furious and exchanged words with a bewildered man standing in an open patio door. The confused man probably pointed to an absentee fisherman who he said had done the yelling.

A second fisherman had parked himself in the motel lobby.

An angry golfer at last came into the lobby and said he had checked into the motel because of its golf course. He said the course was lined with hecklers, and that he wanted his money back.

As the perplexed desk clerk scratched his head, the golfer threatened to call the police.

The desk clerk gave the golfer a refund on his room, plus a ticket for a free round of golf. When the lobby fisherman saw that, he told the rest of us. Satisfied that we'd gotten revenge, we got back on our bus and headed down the highway.

The Blue Bird bus tour of professional bass fishermen was back under way. The press was waiting to report our every word at the next town because we were important and serious sportsmen.

# CHAPTER THIRTEEN

I HAVE 640 acres across federal highway 431 from Tom
Mann's Fish World in Southeast Alabama. My acreage is
immediately next to a national wildlife reserve, thousands of
acres where no hunting is allowed of the alligators, foxes,
deer, and other wildlife. There is also no legalized fishing in
the swamp that stretches a couple of miles to touch Lake
Eufaula.

Eagles soar above my land and the fifteen thousand-acre
reserve. I have put straight poles, twice as tall as utility poles,
on my wilderness. An eagle builds a nest at the top of each
pole every spring.

I've also built eighteen small lakes on the rolling land.

For ten years, I had fishing tournaments there for young-sters. Each child fished eighteen lakes just as a golfer plays eighteen holes. The boy or girl who caught the most fish out of the course was the winner. The youngster got a cash prize and many kinds of fishing tackle. One year, I awarded a bass boat, complete with accessories, donated by Johnny Morris, president of Bass Pro Shops.

The annual tournament had seventy-five contestants its first year. On its tenth and final year, it drew twelve hundred.

I paid for all of the kids' food and prizes. The cost of en-tertaining, feeding, and in some cases awarding twelve hun-dred boys and girls and their parents finally became too much, even though Toyota, Daisy Air Rifle, and Ranger Boats eventually contributed some sponsorship funds.

I still absorbed the majority of the overhead, and the wonderful tournament finally became cost prohibitive for me. It drew untold thousands of dollars into the city coffers. I went to the city fathers to ask them to help me defray the production costs.

During ten years, the city of Eufaula contributed a total of three hundred dollars for the tournaments and the chil-dren, leaving me the lion's share of tens of thousands of dol-lars in overhead.

Later, the city would spend a fortune on alcohol and drug enforcement. I agree with those expenditures. I often wondered, however, how much of that cost could have been prevented if Eufaula had put more money into preventive law enforcement. Young people who love to hold a fishing pole aren't as likely to someday pick up a crack pipe.

The annual tournament was a three-day event, leaving me the rest of the year to stroll my rolling land by myself, usually at sunrise. I have walked my earth daily, unless I was out of town, during my quiet time. I do to this day.

The late country music star Dottie West felt that when one was closer to nature, he was closer to God. I've found that to be true. Sometimes, in the middle of a hectic day, I step outside Fish World and disappear amid the trees and lakes that surround it. My employees don't bother to look for me. That's fine. They couldn't find me anyhow in the nooks and crannies of my rolling land. Most wouldn't want to try, as they'd rightfully fear the thousands of poisonous snakes and hundreds of alligators, some of which could accurately be called man-eaters.

I'm not a man who worries much. I can lie down and fall immediately to sleep for the entire night. I don't take naps, and as I've indicated, I walk the trails I once cleared in my swamp as my therapy. I work inside my retail complex until about eleven P.M. I do that seven days a week, unless I'm traveling.

People ask me how I escape stress, which some feel is the nation's number-one killer, at least indirectly. I avoid it by not acknowledging it. If stress starts to surface in my life, it's usually due to the people in it. Circumstances, of course, are stressful, but many are caused by people other than myself.

So I flee to nature. No plant growth, no breeze, and almost no animal has ever brought me stress. I'm at home with God's creatures and I'm at home with myself—especially while fishing.

Being around animals makes me at ease with myself.

Yet, I'm sometimes torn between the animals I love and the human race that I feel obligated to protect. I never kill a snake unless it's poisonous. I don't want to kill poisonous snakes but want even less to take the chance that a venomous reptile could live to take a human life.

I once came upon a brush pile on my marsh that held eight cottonmouth snakes. The cottonmouth is the most aggressive poisonous snake in America. He'll not only lie silently waiting for his victims, he'll chase a potential victim, including a person.

He can dart faster than most humans can run for a few yards. Then he'll open his mouth to a width twice the size of his diameter and plunge his fangs into the runner's leg. He doesn't have to coil to strike. His victims, if they remain calm, become very sick. If they panic and run, they can die. If anyone were trespassing and were bitten on my land, some of which is three miles to the nearest highway, they might die while panic-stricken and trying to run to civilization after the cottonmouth strike.

With that in mind, I reluctantly killed the eight cottonmouths by hand, using a giant stick. I suppose I should note that most people are bitten by cottonmouths, found in almost every state, because they call attention to themselves. A cottonmouth won't bite you unless you invade his territory, and you usually have to do so with noise. People also make a mistake by seeing a cottonmouth in the woods and clamoring to run from him, or seeing him in the water and slapping the surface to swim away.

If you can remain totally still in the face of an approaching cottonmouth, he'll crawl or swim around you. I've experienced their brush against my leg as I've stood motionless in water while wading and casting for bass.

My conflict between animal and human welfare has surfaced hundreds of times, none more vividly than when I endeavored to protect tourists from a twelve-hundred-pound alligator that I'd seen swimming in my ponds with a deer in its mouth. I'd also seen it carry a Labrador and a calf.

The alligator was obviously to be feared, and he apparently knew it. He began to come out of the wilderness at night when he'd cross 431, a four-lane highway, and crawl onto the mowed grass and pavement of Fish World. If he came when people could see him under the moonlight or security lights, they screamed and ran.

Most alligators aren't aggressive like crocodiles. They don't gravitate toward humans unless humans feed them. It's unlawful to feed alligators on Lake Eufaula, but people do. The alligators are becoming too tame on the lake to suit me. If people don't stop feeding them, I fear a likely tragedy.

I hunted for the great alligator on my acreage, somehow hoping that I didn't find him. He had never frightened me personally.

I found him outside a beaver hut, a stick-and-straw structure that is home to beavers, who leave it to hunt for food. I've spoken previously about my dislike in upsetting the balance of nature. I wish I wouldn't intervene. But I have a soft spot for little animals who are mercilessly devoured by big ones.

Beavers are master architects, and can build a hut that will withstand almost any storm. That's largely due to their huts' solid foundations. People can't see a hut's entry, hidden beneath the water's surface. The beavers come and go through the tunnel that's accessible to alligators.

The big alligator had found the passageway of the beaver hut. Whenever a beaver came out, the alligator would grab him and hold him underwater until he drowned.

Beavers are mammals, and must eventually come up for air. A alligator always drowns his prey before he eats it. The monster was systematically drowning and eating every beaver that lived in the largest beaver hut at Fish World.

Visitors, especially children, were upset when the mammoth reptile surfaced with a baby beaver in his jaws, and then noisily ate the dead and cute animal in front of whoever wanted to watch. Nobody wants to watch something like that. Yet some visitors couldn't take their eyes off it.

As a businessman who wanted to keep tourists happy, and more important, as a conservationist who loves small animals, I was compelled to do something about the recurring massacre.

The easiest thing would have been to shoot the alligator. I refused, however, to kill an animal that was doing no more than what God had intended—consume its natural prey.

Maybe I just took the beavers' side because they're cute and the alligator is ugly. I hope not.

More and more people called for me to take the incredible alligator that was taking small animal life. More and more I told them I would, as long as I didn't have to take his life. People suggested that I sedate the alligator and move him. Others suggested that I catch him and tie his mouth shut, as alligators' reverse jaw muscles are so weak, they can be held shut with one hand. I had all kinds of suggestions that pitted man against the monster. The man in the picture was always me.

The alligator in question was large enough to swallow me to my waist before taking his first chomp.

"We got plenty of alligators around here," I was told. "What's it going to hurt to kill the biggest one? The damn thing is too old and getting too tame. Are you going to wait until it catches a child? Do something."

And so I did.

Henry, an elderly black man, had done manual labor for me for years. I told him I was going to take that alligator by taking away its food. That done, he'd move farther into the swamp, where he'd prey on bottom-feeding fish such as carp and bullfish, and maybe some game fish.

Neither I nor my customers would then have to witness his eating. I said I wouldn't take him from his environment. I'd instead force him deeper into it, for the safety of him and perhaps his eventual human prey.

"How you going to make him move from them beavers, Mr. Mann?" Henry asked.

"By making the beavers move first," I said. "It took about fifty of them to build that hut. I'm going to tear it down by myself."

I told Henry I'd swim underwater to the hut's foundation, and pull branches one by one from the base until the hut, rising ten feet above water, collapsed. The beavers would not rebuild on the same spot, as they naturally rebuild their huts annually at a different location.

I had one problem—a tremendous problem: the alligator. At his size, he could contain enough oxygen to lay on the bottom of my lake for hours without my seeing him. If I swam to the bottom, he could take me about sixteen feet beneath the murky surface. No one would know I was dead until he surfaced with me, or a part of me, in his viselike jaws.

I still could not bring myself to shoot the alligator. I know that sounds corny, but it keeps with the beliefs I've held all my life about protecting animals. But, in order to save the alligator's life, I would have to risk mine.

So I did.

Henry and I waited for hours one day until we saw the monster crawl from the water onto a bank across the small lake. The beaver hut was in the middle.

I handed Henry a rifle.

"I'm going to swim to the beaver hut and then dive to the bottom," I told Henry. "If that alligator sees me, and if he comes after me, I want you to put this rifle barrel under the water and pull the trigger."

I knew that sound, especially blasts, travel underwater.

And so it began. I swam to the middle of the lake and gulped as much air as I could, then turned bottoms-up for my dive toward the base of the entangled hut. I fought to dismantle the hut for as long as I could hold my breath, then I swam to the surface.

I gasped my first inhale of oxygen, but not before spinning in the water to see if the alligator was still on the bank. He was. The water rippled around my eyes. I looked at the hideous giant and it never stopped looking at me. Glaring.

I went back down and had been submerged for perhaps thirty seconds when my ears seemed to split from the reverberation of a rifle shot. I felt terror at sixteen feet.

I shot for the surface, and exhaled hard as my mouth cleared water. Then, perhaps fifty yards away, I saw the alligator swimming slowly and steadily in a deadly path toward me.

I swam hard for shore, and climbed on the bank while the alligator was still about thirty yards behind me.

I had made it with plenty of time to spare.

The ugly reptile thrashed in the water, and swam in a direct line back to his perch on the opposite side of the lake.

"Mr. Tom, I don't think you should fool with this again," Henry said.

But I had seen the underwater opening of the beaver hut. I could see how helpless the animals would be while swimming out of their home directly into the alligator's open jaws.

I couldn't bring myself to stop, not even as I tempted fate more than I ever had.

Once again, I returned to the water. Once again, I dove to the base of the beaver hut. Once again, I frantically tore limb from limb, hoping I'd weaken the infrastructure enough to make the hut collapse, the beavers flee.

Once again, the echo of a rifle blast pierced the dark water.

When I reached the surface, the alligator was closer and was swimming faster. Strangely, as I literally swam for my life, I thought about how I had entered the alligator's world to keep him from eating beavers, and from entering mine. If he took me, it would be because I was trespassing.

But I didn't deserve to forfeit my life while trying to save animal lives, did I? My question was lost to my own pounding of the water as I pulled toward the bank and safety.

That deadly game of hide-and-seek went on all afternoon.

As darkness fell, I was sixteen feet below the water, exhausted and satisfied that I'd made my last dive of the day. I weakly pulled one more branch, and the entire beaver hut gave way. A multitude of branches fell on top of me before they slowly floated to the surface. In the underwater maze, I couldn't see anything, not even something as large as a giant alligator.

But I could hear just fine.

"Bam!" went the rifle.

I tried to pry my body through the puzzle of tangled branches, struggling for the surface and air. My lungs were on fire. Beavers swam furiously around my head and in front of my face.

I couldn't pull my body through the trappings. I honestly thought I was going to drown, but strangely, I didn't think I was going to die. That doesn't make sense. Neither does a lot of my behavior.

The rifle shot was ringing in my ears, but I nonetheless heard myself gasp when I finally broke water. The air tasted as good as it felt.

I looked for the alligator. I couldn't see him. The branches and twigs floated around me, and one was snagged on my face, blocking my vision.

"Mr. Tom! Mr. Tom," I heard Henry scream from the bank.

I still didn't see the alligator. Then I saw two eyes.

In the water, which magnifies size, they seemed to be two feet apart. They seemed to be about fifteen yards from me. I knew they weren't actually that far.

Water also reduces distance.

I spun madly and felt my body warmed by the adrenaline that shot through it. I had often told swimmers not to "slap" the water, as that attracts alligators. I reminded myself of that, then realized there was no danger of my attracting the alligator.

I'd already entered his line of sight since long before the hut collapsed.

I swam as hard and as forcefully as I could. I could hear the water thrashing around me, but not above Henry's screams for me to hurry.

"Faster, Mr. Tom, faster!" he yelled.

Bull alligators, just before they kill, often make a deep and snorting sound, like a Brahma bull. From behind me, I heard the low moan of his snort. It was a belch from the devil.

My arms were heavy and felt like soggy logs. I couldn't do what I had to do, force myself into one more stroke, and then another.

I reached the bank and Henry leapt into the water to pull me ashore. I rose to all fours and dove for land. As I did, I heard the thunderous closing of the man-killing jaws at my back.

He wouldn't come out of the water after me. If he'd been a crocodile, he would have scurried up the bank and eaten me alive.

His jaws closed not a foot behind my leg before I collapsed onto land and safety.

I rolled over and sat upright. I watched him stare at me, as if he were trying to decide whether to do what alligators don't do, leave the water to take me on land. He instead held steady. On my hands and feet, with my back toward the ground, I backed away.

I breathed hard, and watched the beast sink slowly

underwater and out of sight. I didn't see him again until he surfaced and crawled on the bank across the water. He again turned around and stared at me indefinitely.

He could have looked forever. I wouldn't have entered the water again to save any animal lower on the food chain than I was.


THE FLOATING PARTS of the beaver hut had drifted to shore by the next dawn. There was no plant or animal life to indicate that there had once been watery lodging for furry animals in one of my little lakes.

The alligator was not to be seen. Had he already departed because his food supply was gone? I thought not. Alligators are territorial, and I knew he couldn't be moved that easily.

But I knew he'd move eventually.

He did, closer to my corporate offices.

He emerged from the marsh one morning at about two A.M., and silently crossed the four-lane highway into my compound of corporate enterprises at Fish World, as he'd done before. A motorist was speeding north at about seventy miles per hour, the highway patrol later estimated.

The driver hit the giant and prehistoric reptile. The alligator was killed, the car was destroyed, and its driver lived. My attempts to spare the gator's life were dead forever.

# CHAPTER FOURTEEN

THE STATE OF Alabama named me its Small Businessman of the Year in 1978. I and forty-nine other small business-men from as many states were invited to the White House for an award from President Jimmy Carter.

I'd never been to the White House, and marveled at the Lincoln Bedroom and the Oval Office, among other things. I stood in the reception line to meet the president, awaiting my introduction. The president spoke before he was told my name.

"Tom Mann," he said, "I've been a fan of yours for years."

The president had followed the evolution of BASS and

its tournaments. He'd read about me in sports publications and had obtained a copy of my fishing booklet, published the year he became president.

He knew all about my having begun Mann Bait Co. with five dollars, and how Ann and I used the money to buy lead for a mold into which I poured melted lead to shape lures. He recounted how I had personally attached polar-bear hair to my first handmade lures and reminded me of 1959, the year I had finally earned enough to buy an entire polar bear hide for eight hundred dollars.

He also knew where I was from and how I came from a family of ten. Hearing the president tell me about my own life wasn't just flattering, it was overwhelming.

I still didn't understand in 1978 that I could be a celebrity despite the fact that I did not sing, dance, hold public office, or throw a fast ball. I could simply catch fish. I had watched the president as he was introduced to the small businessmen ahead of me. The idea that he knew me, and so much about me, was numbing.

And then the president of the United States, as other honorees waited for his commendation, took time to ask me to take him fishing.

My answer, obviously, was an enthusiastic yes.

Mr. Carter lives in Plains, Georgia, a tiny town about sixty miles from Eufaula. He had left office by the time we finally got to fish, sometime around 1982. He called to confirm our appointment and forgot that there is a one-hour time difference between Alabama and Georgia.

His scheduled arrival time would have therefore put him at my house before daylight. I told him there was no need for that, as the fish would still be sleeping.

I'm a great fan of night fishing. I often put lanterns on my boat to attract insects, which, in turn, attract fish. I have pulled my lures through the insects swarming on the water, and have gotten many strikes from the fish that had been biting on the surface.

That technique works best from about ten P.M. until about five A.M. By six A.M., night fishing becomes predawn fishing. After five A.M., both the bass and the bugs don't seem to be biting, and you're better off waiting until dawn, I explained to Mr. Carter.

Freshwater fish, especially bass, hit what they can see as the sun begins to rise. A top-water lure that makes noise to call attention to itself is your best bet, which is what I told the president.

I later wondered who I thought I was, telling one of the most important men in the world when he could come to my house. But I knew his main interest was catching fish, not seeing me. I wanted to be sure he hooked some big ones.

When he arrived at the home where I still live near Fish World, he told Ann and me he hadn't eaten breakfast. The former commander in chief remedied that by whipping up cheese grits, scrambled eggs, fried eggs and sausage, buttermilk biscuits, and hot coffee.

I may possess the only photo in the world of President Carter standing in a kitchen in front of a cholesterol-laden spread that he'd cooked.

Mr. Carter was a good fisherman but needed some coaching. I felt awkward telling someone of his stature how to do anything, but he insisted he wanted honest lessons.

I pointed out that one mistake he, and others, made was

failing to hold his rod high enough. Mine is always almost perpendicular to the water. If a fish hits my lure, he gets the spring of my rod as reinforcement for the line. When a rod is held straight, it cannot recoil. Hence, the line will often break.

The president had another habit shared by many: He tried to set the hook with his arm, not his wrist. Fishermen who set a hook with their entire forearm set it too forcefully. They often pull the hook from a fish's mouth, sometimes hurting the fish.

I told the president, as I've told others, to set a hook with his wrist. I urged him to turn the crank on his reel a one-half revolution during the set. A hook will catch because of its sharpness, not because of the power behind a pull.

The best way to cut a steak is to move a sharp knife lightly and steadily across the meat. The best way to set a sharp hook is to jerk it lightly but steadily into the fish.

The president caught on rapidly, and soon he was landing most of the fish that hit his lure.

I had often appeared on television programs seen in the president's hometown by the time he and I went fishing. That same year, I signed a contract to become host of my own national fishing show. Suddenly, the fish I caught in Lake Eufaula were being seen as far away as Alaska.

Nothing did more to bolster my popularity, and the popularity of my products, than national television.

I took former President Carter fishing a second time on one of my first national shows, seen on ESPN. He seemed fascinated by my tournament fishing. I was going to fish a tournament later that year whose cash prize, $250,000, was far larger than most of those paid in the mid-1980s.

He couldn't believe that catching more pounds of bass in three days than any other competitor would pay so much. Frankly, neither could I.

I figured my chances of winning were ninety percent, and I told Mr. Carter that, since he had asked.

I didn't win. I came in second or third and won enough money to cover my entrance fee.

Mr. Carter and I talked about the upcoming tournament on my television show, then called *Fishing with Tom Mann*. The show aired on a Saturday morning. That afternoon, ESPN aired another of my shows, this one with a trained orangutan. On Monday morning, ESPN called to tell me that Saturday's show had garnered higher ratings than any outdoor program in its history.

"I guess there is a lot of interest in the former president," I said.

"Who's talking about the president?" the caller replied. "The hit show was with the ape!"

With the exception of Leroy Brown, no animal ever brought me more national attention than the most clever nonhuman mammal I've ever seen. During seventeen years on national television, I've filmed or videotaped shows with celebrities who were household names. They have beefed up my ratings.

Never one to take myself too seriously, I've run programs filled entirely with outtakes, including one in which a hornets' nest fell into the camera crew's boat, flushing hornets around three cameramen, my fishing guest, and me. All of us wound up in the water to protect ourselves from painful stings.

In another show, the camera crew's cables got tangled up

with my boat, and both their boat and mine almost ended up on the bottom of the lake.

People love to laugh at people who are willing to laugh at themselves, and the outtake programs were good for ratings.

The shows in which I was seen catching ten-pound bass were also consistent ratings grabbers.

But I've yet to top the 1986 program I did with a member of the monkey family. Viewers went ape over the ape. Many, who were youngsters at the time, still ask why I don't have the furry guest back on my show.

The answer is simple. He's dead.

Johnny Carson once said that of the thousands of TV shows he'd done, none prompted more queries from viewers than one in which singer Ed Ames threw a hatchet at a human drawing and hit the sketch in the groin.

After eleven years in first run, the most famous *M*A*S*H* program was its final two-hour episode. Alan Alda has said he's still asked about that program.

Just think, my own finest hour in broadcasting is due to an orangutan!

The idea for the show emerged when I went to see Joe Naurd, who'd trained a monkey for a hit movie with Clint Eastwood. When he asked me to come by his place in Florida, I thought we were going to swap celebrity stories or that he might help me recruit some Hollywood stars for my program.

Shortly after I arrived at his office, he told me that someone in the back wanted to meet me.

"He watches your show regularly," Joe said. Then he yelled for Radcliff to join us.

Soon, a towering figure consumed the room. He was fully dressed, he smoked a cigarette, and, after hearing I was Tom Mann, he extended his hand and shook mine firmly.

"Meet Radcliff," Joe said.

"He doesn't know he's an orangutan." He added, whispering, "Don't tell him."

Joe told me that Radcliff loved to fish with a rod and reel and had learned to do so by absorbing the tips I'd given on my show.

This story is already sounding more suspect than the Leroy Brown story.

My claims about Radcliff, however, are supported by videotape seen across the country.

People love to laugh at animals. I don't. I enjoy laughing *with* them, given the kinship I feel with lower forms of life. I believe they actually laugh, although most don't have the facial muscles to smile.

When you look at the loyalty some animals show, you have to wonder why we humans call them "lower forms of life."

Lake Eufaula is filled with Canada geese. Did you know that these geese will mate with only one partner? If that partner dies, the mate will sit by its body until it starves to death or is killed by a predator, human or otherwise.

What is "lower" about that form of loyalty?

Joe and Radcliff arrived in Eufaula about a month after our initial meeting. Joe said Radcliff would ride in my boat and handle his own fishing rig, and that he wanted one like mine.

I guess the most popular rod and reel for beginners is made by Zebco. I gave Radcliff a Zebco, and he gave it back.

"He won't use it," Joe said. "It isn't the same brand as yours, and it's also too weak. Radcliff has the strength of six men in his arms. I suggest you give him a stronger reel, or he'll tear the guts out of the Zebco."

I gave him one of my most expensive and highly technical reels, and he handled it just fine.

I didn't have to show him how to cast or how to retrieve.

"He won't cast a lot at first," Joe said. "He likes to troll before he begins casting."

I thought it was a joke. It wasn't. Radcliff hurled his lure into the water, assumed his position at the back of the boat, and trolled with the precision and patience of a professional. He knew how to hold his rod above the boat motor so his line wouldn't get tangled in the propeller.

I thought I'd seen it all. I hadn't seen anything yet.

Radcliff began to cast, reel, and retrieve his lure. A member of the monkey family was fishing like a man. Radcliff didn't have immediate success. I use a swivel, a metal clip that enables me to quickly change lures without having to tie them to my line. The lures are snapped into place.

Radcliff was unhappy with his lure, and without fanfare dug into my tackle box to retrieve another and attach it to a swivel.

Meanwhile, he periodically reached into my beverage cooler and came up with a soft drink. By himself, he opened the can, then carried it to me. During our outing, I was never without a drink.

I have a "catch and release" policy, as do most professional fishermen. I don't keep a fish unless I intend to eat it. In other words, as you'll notice on my television show, most of the fish my guests and I catch are returned to the water. I kept a few that day for Joe, and, without being shown how, Radcliff used my dip net to lift my fish from the water. He then took them off the hook.

Radcliff caught a nice bass, a five-pounder, I'd estimate. I didn't know it was the largest bass he'd ever caught.

Since he'd been so gracious about fetching my drinks, and pulling in my fish, I thought I'd do something nice for him. I held up his catch, bragged about him to the television audience, then dropped his fish back into the water.

Radcliff became furious. I had thrown away his lifetime catch.

He began to run around the hull and deck of my boat, beating his chest. He then went to the live well, the tank of bubbling water that keeps fish alive, that held the fish I'd caught for Joe.

Radcliff put his arm in the well and, one by one, picked up every fish I'd caught. He waved each in front of me, then threw it back into the water. In the space of a few minutes, he erased my day's take.

Afterward, he continued to get beverages for me and continued to open each of them. But before I could take a swallow, Radcliff would yank the drink from my grip and angrily gulp down the entire thing himself.

Bass fishermen use a main motor to speed from fishing hole to fishing hole. It's powered by gasoline. They use a second motor, a trolling motor, that's powered by a battery. It runs only two or three miles per hour and silently eases a fisherman into the best fishing holes.

Radcliff was apparently unhappy with the spots into

which I was easing us. He poked my sides until I got up from my chair. He then took my seat and began to operate the trolling motor, which requires using one hand and one foot. Radcliff had the movements down to a science.

Radcliff steered us into some real hot spots. We clobbered the fish, thanks to his fish-finding.

Weeks later, Joe decided he would work up a stage show with Radcliff. He did, and Radcliff was scheduled to open at a Las Vegas hotel. Joe even trained a bunch of monkeys to be backup in Radcliff's act. I was invited to the opening.

Neither Joe nor I knew that Radcliff was jealous. He and the monkeys were put into the back of a limousine, while Joe and the driver rode in the front, en route to the opening. Radcliff wanted to be where he thought the important people were, not with the run-of-the-mill monkeys. He banged on the glass that separated the front and the back of the limousine, not stopping until Joe let him up front.

Radcliff thought he was a human being, and thought he should be riding with other humans.

Joe liked beer, and had put a case on ice in the back of the limousine. Radcliff suddenly decided he wanted to ride in the rear with the monkeys. Joe couldn't figure out why the ape had changed his mind.

Joe didn't know that Radcliff, after climbing to the back of the vehicle, passed out beer to the monkeys. He didn't want Joe to hear him open the cans.

Monkeys don't sip a drink, they bolt it. Radcliff opened twenty-four cans of beer and handed them to four fifteen-pound monkeys whose blood alcohol must have reached near-fatal levels.

The Vegas debut was canceled. Each of the backup monkeys had passed out drunk, unable to move and barely able to breathe.

I never had Radcliff on my show again. He was a good fisherman, but like some other celebrities, he was just too temperamental.

# CHAPTER FIFTEEN

I LEFT THE professional bass fishing circuit in 1984. My thirty-minute TV show often took all day to produce, depending on the weather and the distance we had to travel to find a different body of water each week. Sometimes we shot two shows a week, and that meant a trip to two different locations. Television production and my growing businesses left no time for bass tournaments, which sometimes lasted four days.

I had joined the BASS circuit to promote my products. I no longer needed the promotion. I used my lures on television, and that almost brought more business than I could handle with the Eufaula workforce.

I never made much money on the tournament circuit. As I said earlier, I always absorbed my own overhead. Tournament fishing, with rare exceptions, didn't pay as much as it does today.

I had an incredibly successful run as a professional fisherman, and was a consistent winner. I'll always be grateful to Ray Scott and to BASS, as well as to such legendary fishermen as Bill Dance and Roland Martin, who eventually dominated the bass circuit. Bass fishing is a big part of American commerce thanks to Johnny Morris founder of Bass Pro retail outlets. Those men are pillars of what's an international industry and America's favorite personal pastime.

I think I was successful on the tour because while I approached fishing scientifically, I also remembered that it was primarily a sport. I was serious, but not obsessed, about the competition.

I didn't make a big deal out of my departure. I simply finished the tour season and didn't return in 1985. I don't even go to professional fishing tournaments today, unless I'm asked to be a commentator or master of ceremonies. I sometimes fish the annual BASS Legend's Tournament, as I did in 2001.

I didn't win. I wasn't emotionally hurt by that. I participated in the tournament to see old friends and have a good time. I was glad I went and was just as glad to get home to Eufaula and my current undertakings.

I've never been one to live in the past. I also don't live in the future, as I know life carries no guarantees. I try to seize the moment.

People are always asking me what I consider my finest

hour. I tell them it's yet to come. I've done big things on the BASS circuit and in the fishing tackle industry.

I'll do bigger things.


THE MID-1980S were the peak years for my lure and depth-finder companies. Our products were carried by just about every retail store in America where fishing wares were sold. We were also monopolizing the overseas markets and were especially big in Japan.

Plastic worm fishing, because it's a weedless process, is the most popular approach to bass fishing. Southern Plastics Co., my firm that made our plastic worms, ran three shifts a day to keep up with demand.

The Kangaroo Worm, which I invented, is one of the all-time best sellers. Its name is pretty self-explanatory. This lure has a pouch that resembles a kangaroo's attached to the worm's underside. A fisherman may purchase one of my cream scents, whose ingredients are a secret, to stuff inside the worm's pouch. The scents draw bass to the worm, a natural bait.

It was a good idea whose time had come, and continues to come over and over.

I haven't mentioned much about my seven brothers and sisters because significant discussion of that many siblings could make for a separate book. Most have had their own successful vocations or careers, and I'm proud of their success.

My brother Don was drawn to my interests. Don loved to fish and was fascinated by lure design. We were compatible because he shared my approach to employee management.

He was happy-go-lucky and informal in his role as a supervisor.

We made it a point to walk the assembly line during the various shifts. We called the employees by name and asked about their welfare. If someone had a grievance, we listened.

Don and I were not above giving our best employees financial help out of our own pockets. Many of the employees were not above going that extra mile for us when filling a big order.

I think all our companies had a family atmosphere. I hope some of the workers saw Don and me as father figures who didn't administer unreasonable discipline. We never fired unless it was for theft or complete failure to make a reasonable effort to work.

Don was my brother and everybody's friend.

He and I also shared the same idea about persistence. When he thought he was right, he wouldn't quit the pursuit of his goal.

The Occupational Safety Hazard Administration once visited all of our factories and found no safety violations. Don felt the inspector was uneasy, and seriously thought the guy was anxious about what he'd tell his supervisor. It wouldn't be simple for him to explain how he could walk across thousands of square feet in front of hundreds of workers and not find a single violation of the federal safety code.

But Don ran a tight and efficient ship. He knew his work place met federal standards.

The inspector fined us $125 anyhow.

"He's doing that just to justify his trip to Eufaula from Montgomery," Don said. "I'm not going to pay the fine. I'll fight it in court."

I suspected it would cost us much more than $125 in time and attorney fees to fight the fine. But Don had his principles, and he wouldn't be shaken from them.

Don arrived in court, where the government's lawyer moved to have the hearing set for another date.

"I'm ready now!" Don said. "I've come all this way!"

He pointed out that he was one man who was ready for a charge levied by the government, whose ranks were filled with thousands of employees.

The judge, also a government worker, ruled against Don. A continuance was granted.

Later, the government's attorney called Don to ask if he'd agree to pay one half the fine and call that a settlement.

"No!" he said. "I'll be back in Montgomery to tell the court why I shouldn't have to pay *anything*."

By that time I was sure the inspector who gave Don a citation wished he'd given it to someone more passive.

"I want to be in court and I *will* be in court," Don added.

A day or two later the lawyer called. He told Don that if he went to court, he'd go alone. The lawyer said the government had decided to drop the fine. Don couldn't sue the government regarding a fine that was no longer imposed.

The government lawyer said the decision to withdraw the proposed penalty was based on the judge slated to hear the lawsuit. The counselor claimed that the judge had found the petition to be frivolous, but Don didn't believe that.

He knew he'd been unfairly fined, and he felt the government didn't want to hear fair and persuasive evidence that he was sure would prove his contention. Don had photographs and had even subpoenaed witnesses as part of his evidence.

He spent a few thousand dollars to beat a $125 fine. But he kept his ideals intact, and to him, that was priceless.

It was to me too. My pride in him was even more invaluable.

Don was the sole inventor of one of the most important machines in the history of the various Tom Mann enterprises.

We were still making plastic worms by hand and from molds. The tedious process enabled us to keep up with demand, but not much more. As a result, we struggled to get ahead on our inventory.

Then Don invented a plastic worm machine that is about as flawless as my Humminbird. I won't go into the technical aspects, I'll just say that it turned raw plastic into a perfectly shaped and detailed replica of a live worm. It shot the finished product onto a table about as fast as a pistol could be fired.

You can imagine how many plastic worms we were able to produce when we got the machines on line.

That did it. Our business went over the top. And I, and the many Eufaula residents on our payroll, had Don to thank. Locally, we were called the Mann Brothers, and Don's name was regularly mentioned in the same sentence as my own. That delighted me.

He had money in the bank, a wonderful family, the love of the community, and more. He defined the American dream, as he had risen from the same poverty-stricken conditions to become one of the state's, and the nation's, top small-business executives.

And he was more. He was the lieutenant every corporate president needs. Don could handle my conglomerate in my absence. When I needed a break from the pressure, I could leave all my businesses with Don.

I had made many lakes on my property, as I've indicated, by digging them myself. I used to work for weeks on a bull-dozer, digging the depths and shallows, as well as the dams for the lakes. I did it as a hobby until word spread about my ability to build a lake that would sustain abundant fish life.

The next thing I knew, I was involved in another venture. I didn't necessarily want to convert my lake work into an enterprise. I wanted to keep it a psychological hideout. But people continued to press me about building lakes. I finally agreed to design and dig ponds for twenty thousand dollars each. I suspected that would discourage some of those clamoring for my services.

I was wrong. I had so many requests that I could have dug ponds full-time for a lucrative living. Instead, I eventually made a videotape about how to design and dig a pond and sold it on my television show.

Don wanted no part of my pond undertakings and thought I should do *something* in my life that carried no price tag. He said I needed the time away from the pressure to perform, and I suppose he was right.

But as Don knew, I had a long memory. You think you can never have enough money as an adult after you've been virtually penniless as a child.

I nonetheless had taken Don's advice one afternoon when I retreated to my bulldozer to work on a new lake—my lake. I was lost in the sound of the John Deere's purr and the smell that arises from freshly moved earth.

Birds were landing around me to retrieve the insects I uncovered as I herded the tractor back and forth in its own steel tracks. In my seat atop the bulldozer, I was on top of the world.

Suddenly, I spotted my wife dashing toward me. I pulled the throttle and cut the engine to an idle.

I had trouble hearing her as she yelled up at me, still in the bulldozer's seat.

I asked her to yell louder.

And so she did. And her voice carried across the woods. For me, it would echo forever in my mind.

"There's been an accident with Don," she said.

I couldn't believe my next two questions.

"Is he dead?" I asked.

She nodded yes.

"Was it suicide?" I asked.

"Yes," she replied.

I came off the tractor, wondering just what in the world had happened and why I had asked what I had. I think siblings have an intuition about each other's welfare.

"Don's dead," Ann repeated.

"How? When?" I think I asked, or at least I tried to.

Don had gone to the plant on a Sunday morning when no one else was there. Alone, he put a gun to his head.

People have asked me to explain why ever since that horrible day in 1986. I can't, as I've been unable to explain it to myself.

I went to Don's funeral but not to his grave. I haven't been there to this day. I also saw a psychiatrist for the first and only time in my life.

The doctor told me about mood swings and chemical imbalance. I learned that Don's brain probably had a shortage of a natural chemical that keeps most people happy. I was asked if he had been happier on some days than on others. I thought everybody was that way.

I was asked to recall Don's childhood, and I remembered how he was a perfectionist. No matter how well he did, he wanted to do better.

I had simply thought he was an overachiever, and I admired that about him. I don't appreciate people who do things halfway.

But then I began to realize how he was always driven to be the best, even after he'd done his absolute best.

I remembered how he'd fish a bass tournament with two hundred entrants and finish in the top twenty. People would be congratulating him as he scolded himself for not having placed higher.

I remembered the text of one of two final notes he wrote—one to me. Although Southern Plastics, the company I'd entrusted to him, was doing an unprecedented volume of business, Don was not satisfied. In his last correspondence to me, he apologized because the company was not doing better.

The words cut me like a dagger. I merely had to read about Don's imagined failure. He had to live with it.

And so he chose to live no longer.

At the funeral, I listened to each word that was said, but I heard little.

I can't tell you what hymns were sung or what Bible verses were read. A preacher struggled to make sense of what was the most painfully senseless thing I've ever endured.

People who commit suicide have no idea how they damage the lives of those who love them. It doesn't matter that the victims don't love themselves.

For the first time in my life, I fell into genuine depression. I'm not talking about the sadness or blue moods that would naturally go with the loss of a loved one. I'm talking about my total loss of the winning spirit, something that has been as instinctive for me as breathing.

I had made my work my life, and I no longer cared to work. I suspect that some of my loved ones interpreted that to mean I'd lost the will to live.

Not entirely so, but I was down. Very down. I paid a terrible price. And I'm paying to this day.

I'm going to make a long story short because I don't see the point in outlining every wrinkle in the legal maneuvering, and because it's still too distressful to talk about.

But I wound up selling my companies for a much lower fee than they were worth. I could either sell them or lose them. Don and I had built a string of international businesses from one business whose origin in my kitchen could not have been more humble. I had spoken about Eufaula so much on national television that some folks said I did more to put the city on the nation's recreational and tourism map than anyone else. I had sold stock to twenty people in one company, upon its inception, for twenty thousand dollars each. Each of those twenty people saw their stock evolve into a one-million-dollar holding. I had employed people who had raised their families, many putting their children through school, on the salaries I paid.

I had done it with a tireless spirit. Nothing, but nothing, could eliminate my determination during the formative years. I had carried that kind of gumption with me into the companies' best years.

Then, with the quickness of the discharge of a bullet, I lost my attitude, the cornerstone of all I had done.

I knew how to fight to keep what was mine. I just didn't know how to make myself want to fight anymore.

My brother was dead.

I received an undisclosed lump sum, and as I said, ensuing royalties from the sale of my companies. Eventually, it would all be spent. And a boy from Penton, Alabama, whose creations as a man had rocked the fishing world, would fall from financial grace.

After some time, I started designing new lures: the Kangaroo Lure System, the 3D Lure System, and the Pogo Line of lures. I am still designing lures today.

# CHAPTER SIXTEEN

I DID A lot of fishing after Don's death, and I did it for the right reason—because I wanted to. I wasn't seeking prize money or trying to call attention to whatever lures I used.

The struggle to take, and to keep, my companies from me was not a short one, and the recurring court sessions seemed interchangeable. I sued to recover what I had sold too cheaply, and I felt that some defense witnesses lied when they testified. I ultimately lost the case along with my companies, which I had built on a shoestring budget to their multimillion-dollar annual gross.

I essentially started over, with plenty of seed money and more than thirty years' experience manufacturing fishing equipment. I founded new companies that offered innovative lures and pressed forward with my television show.

As I used my newly invented lures on my show, I told viewers they could buy them from Tom Mann Lure Co. and recited an 800 number. I also told them what retailers carried the new line. People responded with their dollars.

I handled all the money I made from my new companies and the royalties I derived from the sales of my old. I never built up to the volume of business I once had because Don wasn't there to help me and because I didn't want the responsibility and stress that I'd faced as a younger man.

Getting my products to the public, however, wasn't the struggle it had been when I first hawked them from a cigar box and traveled a route of gas stations. I had credibility, thanks to the mark I'd made as a professional fisherman and as the inventor of so many lures.

And as I said, when I wasn't working I went fishing.

That relaxation wasn't entirely without peril. Being out of doors is almost always relaxing. But on occasion it can be nothing less than life-threatening.

I was fishing one day with a buddy, when a violent thunderstorm began to build. I could see lightning streak across the sky about fifty miles away, and I could hear the low rumble of thunder. The sky grew as dark as a moonlit night.

I knew it was time to lay down my rod, as rods can attract lightning. I was just about to put the pole aside, when it began to emit a sound—a low hissing, or singing.

I discovered I couldn't open my hand to loosen my grip. Then I felt the hair on the back of my neck literally begin to rise.

I guess that electricity, through static or other atmospheric conditions, was beginning its subtle pass through my body. I'm not sure. I simply knew I had to get the pole out of my hand and get myself off the water. I dove for my boat motor, which, in those days, was started by a button.

As I leaned over the engine, the pole still stuck to my rigid hand, my body began to feel very warm. I was scared.

Suddenly, a bolt of lightning hit the tip of my rod and shot through my torso. All my depth finders and other electronic equipment were knocked out of service, as the strike traveled through me and into my fiberglass craft. I was a human conduit for lightning.

My grip locked harder, and I fell toward the steering wheel, determined to slam the idling motor in gear. My buddy and I collided as the boat rocked and reeled. The steering wheel was rubber and so were the soles of my shoes. A doctor later told me that having my hand and feet against rubber is all that saved my life.

Addled and becoming unable to function, I began to lose consciousness. My buddy drove the boat toward the dock as I lay on its bottom. I passed out for thirty minutes, my friend later estimated.

He traveled about twenty miles across water before I came to. I remember thinking that I now knew what it would feel like to be electrocuted. Still on the floor of the boat, I felt the thump of waves on the underside of the hull. I stared upward, watching the clouds, marveling at how fast I seemed to be traveling as the clouds seemingly stood still.

That's the kind of thing a child ponders. Memories of childhood and other parts of life pass through your mind when you're close to death, I've been told. I've never thought about just how close I really was because, as I've said previously, I never expect to die. That's not exactly right. Consciously, I know I'll someday die. But I've never thought that I've breathed my last, no matter how dire my circumstances.

While peering upward in a haze, I thought about Don. I felt his spirit with me, and I wondered what he thought about my situation. I thought about my family, and I thought about that first time I was hit by lightning, while making plastic worms in my basement many years earlier.

About forty-five minutes after the second lightning strike in my life, I struggled to my feet. My buddy wanted to continue toward shore and medical attention for me.

I told him I'd see a doctor after I finished fishing.

Despite his admonitions, he and I returned to the greater lake and to casting. When she later learned of this, my wife was not amused because I hadn't gotten immediate treatment, especially after she heard that one side of my body had been numb for more than an hour.

But I knew that in time the fish would bite, as they often do after a storm. And I knew that time heals all wounds, even from lightning strikes. I thought that time itself could do as much for me as a doctor, and I chose to spend my time chasing fish in case it actually *was* my time to go. If I were going to leave this world, I was determined to leave it while fishing. But once again, in my mind death seemed like it was for everyone else but me.

Others in my family don't agree with my theory about my defying destiny. My wife even hid my fishing gear a time or two afterward whenever the weather looked threatening.

ABOUT THAT SAME time, on weekends, I began to appear at boat and travel shows. The promoters held them mostly in the winter, as they still do. They paid me to set up a booth with big letters that spelled out the name of my fishing show. I've appeared under marquees that said *Tom Mann Outdoors, Fishing with Tom Mann,* or whatever I happened to title my show during a given year.

I discovered that participating in the shows was easier than doing the one-night speaking engagements I mentioned earlier. Sometimes the show promoters paid me to give fishing seminars, and that was easy. Simply answering questions constituted much of my presentation. I stood inside my booth during the rest of the time as thousands of people passed by.

People who don't fish often think the majority of tackle is sold in the summer. That isn't true. Summer is when people use the tackle they buy in the winter. The slowest-selling months are July and August.

At those giant winter shows, some of which attract 250,000 spectators a day, I spread out pamphlets, brochures, and catalogs about my lures in front of me. The boat and tackle shows proved to be the best one-on-one contact with consumers I'd ever experienced. I gave them a handshake, a smile, an autograph, and the paperwork needed to order my new lures from one of my new companies.

In the past, I had gone to the people to build my companies. The boat and tackle shows brought the people to me. As they waited in line, they watched silent footage of one of my television shows.

They waited attentively. When they finally had their turn to approach, they never failed to ask what lure I was using when I caught the fish on the show they'd seen while waiting.

I love that kind of direct marketing. I love to sell and to listen to people. They'll tell you exactly what they like, and don't like, about a lure. I combine their feedback and my own imagination to modify my creations. Change is always constant with me, as it should be with anyone who tries to satisfy the revolving buying habits of the American public.

Fishermen also are not shy about voicing other requests, some of them unrelated to tackle. I've been asked to pose for Polaroid snapshots with old women who'd then ask me to sign the picture to the "prettiest girl in the world" or something similar.

BY THE EARLY 1990s my new lure companies had gotten about as big as I wanted. I wanted to run a number of small businesses. I also wanted to market overseas. I was doing all of that.

I didn't, however, want to oversee three shifts a day working at numerous plants. I could have done that, perhaps, if I'd had help. But I didn't want to hire the help that can breed the headaches that go with a small empire. I had been there, done that, and bought the souvenir T-shirt.

I remained a business with worldwide distribution through independent distributors. I didn't try to handle international distribution from my own facilities in Eufaula.

I never employed more than forty people as I rebuilt my career.

It's no secret that success breeds success. It also attracts those who want to be successful themselves. I was swamped in the mid-1990s by bright young engineers who wanted to show me how to streamline mass production.

I didn't need streamlining. I was making and selling as many lures as I wanted to. I nonetheless gave the young people an audience. I'm willing to consider advice from any source, which I think is another secret to success. An open mind is a productive mind.

Most of the talented young people addressed my assembly line, and most suggested that I install flat conveyor belts. They showed me charts and graphs about how much product I could move from worker to worker.

I weighed their suggestions but never implemented any of them. I let my labor force grow to my desired optimum. They produced an astonishing ten thousand finished and boxed lures a day by using another bicycle chain in lieu of a flat conveyor belt per se. I taught employees how to hang a lure on the electrically powered chain and how to do their respective jobs as it passed by, just as I had with those at my first mass-production plant about a quarter of a century earlier.

"A bicycle chain is a very primitive approach to mass production," one engineering whiz pronounced.

"It sure is," I said, "and it doesn't break down, it's cheap to build, and it's proven to be effective."

"You're bringing your old techniques to your new business," he said in an accusing tone.

"You're right," I agreed, smiling. "I'll also bring something else that's old to my new businesses."

"What?" he asked.

"Success," I said.

The public was buying lures from Mann Bait Co., mistakenly thinking I still owned it, and from the new Tom Mann Lure Co., correctly thinking I owned that too. My name, or my official emblem, was on the products turned out by every company I owned or had owned. I had income from all, and at one time, there were as many as six.

I had been emotionally destroyed and economically stressed in the wake of my brother's death and the unethical takeover it prompted. But I had proven that no one could keep a good man, or at least a man with good intentions, down forever.

Before the decade's end, I'd also add another enterprise to Tom Mann's Fish World, building the last grocery store and gas station that motorists pass before heading north out of Eufaula toward Georgia. More than nineteen thousand cars, carrying more than forty thousand people, would pass the facility each day by 2000, according to the state highway department.

My life and career continued to move decidedly forward.

My renewed success apparently disappointed a lot of those who'd taken advantage of me when I was down. I think they wanted me to take what amounted to a token payment and my remaining royalties and go away. My presence in a small town like Eufaula was a reminder of what I was doing anew. It was also a harsh reminder of what some folks had done to me in the past.

I didn't want to build my new businesses entirely with my own money. I had borrowed to build my first group of companies and had repaid my loans only to borrow and repay again. If you can invest your money for a higher rate of return than lenders are charging, you're unwise not to borrow for expansion.

The city of Eufaula continued to decline to underwrite, even in part, the activities I sponsored that brought commerce to town.

"We don't have the money to help you sponsor your next event," city officials told me repeatedly.

A few days earlier, I'd read a newspaper story about the city's throwing as much as twenty-five thousand dollars behind a touring fishing event unrelated to me. Few, if any, of those events drew as many tourists to Eufaula as Tom Mann–sponsored productions had attracted. Did the city's sponsorship of outsiders while neglecting me make me angry? No, but it hurt my feelings.

The 1990s saw my popularity expand nationally and overseas, while it diminished in my hometown. I was controversial in Eufaula.

Few men are self-made, and fewer are self-made and successful. I had been self-made and successful during two go-rounds. A lot of people didn't expect me to rebound, and almost no one in town expected me to do it so quickly.

I was the black sheep among Eufaula's prosperous and a rebounded hero of its working class, to which I was once again providing employment. Many people who'd worked in my old companies wanted to work in my new. I couldn't hire all of them and maintain my position of controlled growth.

Twenty years earlier, my wife and I had been invited to all the right social events in Eufaula. I never enjoyed going to most of the phony affairs. But I was no longer invited after the wives of the men who'd acquired my old companies became chairpersons.

That was fine with me.

To this day, I eat almost daily at one of Eufaula's mom-and-pop restaurants, built and patronized by working folks. The owners and customers always make me feel welcome.

Not a day passes without one of them telling me how they appreciate what I've done for the city. Many times, their grown children thank me for the college educations they indirectly derived from me.

# CHAPTER SEVENTEEN

ALTHOUGH I INVOLVED my wife and children in my businesses while building my first fortune, the kids eventually wanted to pursue their own interests. I understood.

As I embarked on my second career, I sometimes continued to wish that I'd not let work take me from my children, especially when they were teenagers.

Absentee parenthood is a mistake, one made by too many people. They're always going to *start* doing more with their kids. Once past their early years, kids move toward their own interests. If you don't move with them, they'll move emotionally away from you. Both offspring and parent are the ultimate losers, and the parent probably could have prevented it.

The majority of my television viewers are family people. They've faced some of the same struggles I have faced. Many have learned from their mistakes, the best teacher. The following words offer an opportunity to learn from another's mistakes—mine.

I've had four children, all of whom have been been a blessing to Ann and me. But if I had to do it over, there are some things I'd do differently. For one, I wouldn't give them as many material things. I bought each child a car, and bought one several. I let each live with a spouse in one of my houses free of charge.

I've received all kinds of mail during my career. Most of the correspondence, obviously, had to do with fishing. But people have also asked for advice about marriage, finances, and other personal subjects. I guess my viewers consider me family, since I enter their homes via television twice a week.

One of the most frequent topics of correspondence, besides fishing, regards parenthood. My rule of thumb today: Don't give your children too many "things," give them yourself. I wish I had given fewer things and more of myself to my own kids.

Some of my children have had disappointments they might not have had if I'd been more of a presence during their early years. I think I was particularly wrong in my approach to my son, Tommy, who I wanted to follow in my tracks. It was hard for him to fill my shoes.

I taught Tommy to fish when he was young. He became very good very quickly, and I put him on the BASS professional tour when he was only sixteen. He might have become a champion had it not been for the pressure. I realized years later that he was there mostly because I, not him, wanted that. I didn't fully understand years ago what he was talking about when he cited pressure. I do now.

I've learned about the famous-father syndrome and how it's difficult to be your own man while constantly being compared with your dad.

The most dramatic example of this I can think of involves Hank Williams Jr., whose autobiography was made into a movie. The book and movie recount the rudeness of an adoring public who wanted Hank Jr. to be a clone of his daddy, the most legendary country singer/songwriter of all time—the hillbilly Shakespeare. People didn't always care about Hank Jr.'s music. They cared about how well he could perform his daddy's.

To make a long story short, as Hank himself has said, it all became too much for him and in 1972 he attempted suicide by ingesting a bottle of Darvon. He was rushed to an Alabama hospital, where his stomach was pumped and his life was saved.

As a physician stood over Hank Jr., he itemized the entertainer's risks in trying to fulfill everyone's wishes but his own.

"You've been programmed to walk like Hank Williams, to talk like Hank Williams, to sing like Hank Williams," the doctor said. "Now," he continued, "you're going to wind up like Hank Williams—dead!"

Hank Williams died at age twenty-nine of a drug-induced heart attack. His drinking and drug binges are almost as legendary as his music.

To this day, people still compare Hank Jr. with his father.

But not for long, at least not in Junior's presence. He won't stand for it.

Fishing fans used to compare Tommy Mann with Tom Mann when my son was just barely old enough to shave. The comparison was as unfair as it was difficult for Tommy. The fans would actually become *angry* with Tommy if he didn't win a bass tournament. They thought there was magic in the name Mann and that all Tommy had to do was drop his lure into the water to automatically weigh fish.

Don, my late brother, went through similar comparisons, to a lesser degree. Perhaps that played a part in his suicide.

I learned to fish as a boy with the help of my dad and Uncle Alvin, who were there for me because they weren't away at fishing tournaments or working eighteen-hour days to expand their empires.

Tommy's critics didn't realize the pressure of tournament fishing. Even I never understood how stressful it could be until I encountered it personally. And I had no one's expectations to meet but my own.

I was wrong to put Tommy on the tournament trail when he was so young. The fans were wrong to compare him with me and to demand that he catch fish.

Tommy Mann will forever be *my* son. I wish the public and he would let him become his *own* man.

Disillusioned, Tommy withdrew from professional fishing. I then offered him a job running one of my companies on two occasions. He was too young to be offered so much. He didn't want to work in my shadow. I understand that now. He backed away from executive positions in two companies, each of which would have paid him a handsome salary and then a cool million dollars when the companies were sold.

At sixteen, like most teenagers, Tommy was a long way from finding himself. He instead found a bottle.

An off-duty member of the Alabama Highway Patrol gave Tommy his first alcohol. The trooper wanted to have a drink with Tom Mann's son. No one ever became a heavy drinker without taking his first drink. I'd like to meet the trooper, a paid public servant who was supposed to discourage underage drinking, and ask him if he's proud of how he influenced Tommy. I'd like to ask if he's given alcohol to the kids in his own family.

Tommy became a victim of running with the wrong crowd. The first member of that crowd belonged to the Alabama Highway Patrol.

In time, Tommy drank too much every night. In more time, he drank too much every night and every day.

Tommy knows that. He's been in drug and alcohol rehab many times. He'd be the first to tell you that he approves of my revealing this if it will help one person avoid substance abuse.

But again, when Tommy was young, I focused on the career and the material things I wanted for him.

What have I learned?

For starters, if I could raise my children again, I wouldn't buy a single one an automobile. That's a radical statement in an era of personal mobility.

Parents too often use television or home computers as electronic baby-sitters when their children are young. When the children are older, and having problems, the parents try to soothe their own guilty consciences by buying their kids cars.

The child then drives himself down the highway on the route toward irresponsibility. With the exception of a house, an automobile is the most significant purchase most people ever make. Owning a car is a young person's first marked responsibility.

When they're children, they may be expected to clean their rooms. If they don't, the house doesn't fall down. If they don't maintain their car, however, its engine might blow up, its tires might blow out, and the entire notion of taking care of personal property will likely be blown to the wind.

You can "do" and "do" for your children to the point where their ability to "do" for themselves is lessened.

I've learned a lot about human life from having watched animal life. There are similarities and lessons for all of us. The smartest and most self-sufficient bird I've ever seen, for example, is the eagle. She doesn't fly in a flock, she doesn't eat another bird's leftovers or the remains of a hunter's prey. She is fed by her own devices. An eagle never forms a nest in one previously occupied by another bird or other animal. She builds her own and can build one without any support from adjacent branches.

When her eaglets are big enough to fly, they are eased out of the nest. They're not cast out, they're ushered gently and they don't even realize it.

The mama will gradually begin picking out the tiny feathers that were woven into the nest to make it soft. As she removes more of her down, the nest becomes more and more prickly for her babies. In an effort to comfort themselves, they eventually attempt to fly from the nest, into the clouds.

She flies under them, not above them and not with them. They don't get to ride her back. She catches them on it only if they fall.

I should have let my kids find their own way earlier in life. I should have been there only if they fell. I'm proud of what some have done. I'm very proud, although I'll bet some of the more accomplished wish they had done things differently or done them earlier.

They didn't because their mom and I were too protective and too generous. Our kids eventually paid the price.

As they look back, they might think we deprived them of lessons in responsibility and enabled misconceptions about life's realities.

We certainly didn't teach Tommy to take responsibility when it comes to cars. He's parked a car with a flat tire beside the road, then left it there for weeks. My ranting for him to pick up the stranded automobile did neither of us any good.

"I'll go get it," he'd say. "I'll go get it later."

"You'd better," I'd reply. "I'm sure not going to buy you another one."

But I usually did, often after the abandoned car had been stolen. I was wrong to buy Tommy another.

Tommy, meanwhile, continued to work now and then at jobs he eventually quit. He went through the failed-marriage bit, complete with child rearing in a motherless home. His daughter often faced her teenage years with a father who might or might not be at home. Even when he was physically present, he often was drinking or strung out on cocaine. Miraculously, after years of using the latter, he whipped the habit through willpower. The doctors told me that was extremely rare.

He suffered a serious health mishap—twice. The second incident, in 1998, was much like the first ordeal.

I was dispatched to the hospital, where I was told Tommy was dead on arrival due to liver failure. Once on the scene, however, I learned that a doctor had revived Tommy while his mother and I anguished in a waiting room cold enough to hang meat.

Finally allowed to see Tommy, I went into an operating room, where he was shaking with cold and fighting for his breath.

A second doctor was contacted and said he was on the way. An hour later, he still hadn't arrived.

I'm no doctor, I'm a father. I knew my son was going to die if he didn't get adequate medical attention.

Out of desperation, I confronted the doctor's aide who said he couldn't force the doctor to get to the hospital any faster. I said I couldn't either, but my boy was dying.

The aide got on the phone again. This time the doctor said he'd talk him through a procedure to insert a tube into Tommy's nose to determine if he was bleeding internally.

Tommy's coughing up blood is the reason he'd been taken to the hospital. I didn't have to be a doctor and I didn't have to thread a tube down his nose to know my son was bleeding internally.

The aide nonetheless struggled to get the tube into Tommy's nostrils. Tommy, meanwhile, was becoming sober and out of his mind with pain. I've undergone the same procedure, and it's the most painful thing I've ever experienced.

Snake bites and lightning strikes are walks in the park by comparison.

Tommy violently resisted the young aide, who continued to struggle to insert the tube. My wife couldn't watch and left for the waiting room, where she prayed without ceasing.

"I can't do anything with your son!" the exhausted aide finally told me. "He's too strong, and he's resisting too much. I can't get any help. I can't do anything!"

"He's dying!" I repeated yet again.

The aide repeated that he couldn't get the medical help he needed.

"You've got help!" I shouted. "Get back over here. You and I are going to get this tube down his nose."

Now, the reason for getting a tube inside Tommy was to drain blood so that he wouldn't drown in it.

I'm surprised I wasn't arrested for practicing medicine without a license. I restrained Tommy as he fought me with the strength of a yearling bull. I leapt on top of the hospital table, forced his hands behind his back, and held him down with all the power I could muster.

Tommy's screams could be heard by people up and down the hall.

The doctor himself arrived—two hours after Tommy's admission to the emergency room.

He walked to Tommy's side, examined him, and finally went to work.

He told my wife and me he didn't think Tommy would live until morning and asked us to sign a release that would allow removal of Tommy's life support system.

I asked the doctor if my son had even the slightest prayer.

"Yeah," the doctor said, hesitating.

I said I would sign nothing.

The doctor said he had tied off about fifty of Tommy's veins to lessen the internal bleeding.

"If he lives, he'll be in a coma for three or four days," the doctor said.

It was Monday.

"If he makes it until Thursday, he's got a chance," the doctor said.

Ann and I sat by Tommy's bedside daily, from almost daylight until dark. We returned home only to catch a few hours' sleep.

At noon Thursday, Tommy sat upright in bed as if nothing had happened.

"What's going on?" he asked.

I was overjoyed that he was alive. I was furious at him for what he'd put himself, and us, through. Eventually, I was just as mad at myself for all my shortcomings as a father.

As of this writing, Tommy is in another state, trying to get sober.

He needs money and has asked for twenty dollars a day. I can't send it. He'll use it, I fear, to buy whiskey.

We've been down this road before.

Nothing has gotten him permanently off alcohol. Once I even conspired with a judge to sentence Tommy to a prison hospital, where he couldn't get booze. The judge thought that several months of forced sobriety would make Tommy well.

Tommy has been through so much. Why would anyone who'd been down that rocky road still want to travel it?

He's got a disease. It's called alcoholism. That's why I don't turn him away.

I mean, I wouldn't turn my back on my son if his disease were cancer. I won't turn him away because he's afflicted with alcoholism.

Is it genetic? Is it psychological? I don't know. I only know Tommy has the disease and that he wouldn't have it if he hadn't had that first drink. And he might not have the disease if he had the self-esteem that comes from earning his own way, instead of having material things given to him by an absentee and willfully overworked dad.

But it's still Tommy's disease, and only Tommy can whip it. His family can support him, but ultimately he'll have to do it alone. So far, he hasn't.

And so my haunting question remains: Where would Tommy be today if I had been with him more when he was young? The *things* I gave him were just reminders of my absence.

The kinds of questions I ask myself are questions you won't have to answer if you never have to ask them.

Be there for your kids as a person, not merely as a provider.

# CHAPTER EIGHTEEN

DURING THE 1990S, my fishing show aired on ESPN and on the Nashville Network, the coast-to-coast cable channel that offers full-time country music, the most commercially accepted of the decade. The station had a built-in audience of youthful viewers who wanted to see superstars such as the most successful recording artist of the '90s, Garth Brooks, and country music's biggest-selling female recording artist, Reba McEntire. A lot of young people kept their television dial tuned to TNN and wound up watching me fish.

That might explain, in part, why so many young adults have taken up sportfishing.

Not since fans dared me to catch a great white shark

while standing on dry land have I received as many challenges as I received during the '90s about fishing.

People actually challenged me to train a bass while it was in its native environment.

I am probably the only professional fisherman, active or retired, to claim that bass can be trained. You can train them as surely as you can train some house dogs.

My television audience knew about my success with Leroy Brown and pointed out that I had trained him to do astonishing feats while he was in captivity.

"Let's see you do it with bass that are in the wild," they wrote.

It isn't hard to train bass when you think like—make that outthink—the fish.

It's no secret that bass prefer live food, although they often kill before they consume it, as I've said previously. I've always made artificial lures that when pulled through the water simulate life.

In most parts of the country a fisherman can buy a dozen live minnows more cheaply than he can buy one artificial lure. Bass love live minnows. But minnows die, and bass are not naturally drawn to dead minnows.

"I can't afford to buy two or three dozen live minnows every time I go fishing," people often wrote to me. "Do you suppose you could come up with a technique for catching bass with dead minnows?"

I did. Fishing with dead minnows is an economical way to fish, as many bait shops will give them away free.

Consumers who use dead minnows don't help my artificial lure business. I'm not doing myself any favors by telling how to catch bass with something I didn't make. But, in the interest of cultivating even more interest in bass fishing, I'll explain how live bass are taken on minnows that are not.

The bass is the only freshwater fish in the world that can be trained. He's as smart as some mammals. And he's as territorial as he is bright.

Don't fish by waiting for the bass to come to you. You can hunt him more rapidly than he'll hunt for you and your bait. How do you find him? By looking for structure, by seeking bait fish visible on the surface, by bouncing an anchor off the bottom of the lake until you find a ledge, by affixing lanterns to your boat or dock at night to attract insects that attract bass, by using a depth finder and by all the other ways I've previously mentioned.

Once you find bass, throw a live minnow minus a hook into the water. They'll hit the minnow. Throw another and another, as a feeding bass will often attract still more bass that will also feed.

Go back the next day. Unless there's been a drastic change in weather, the bass will likely be in the same place at the same time. Feed them more live minnows.

You may not see the bass strike the first minnows you drop in the water. Soon, however, they'll learn that the minnows are falling from above, and they'll begin to strike closer to the surface, especially at dusk or dawn. You'll eventually see them hit.

In a matter of days, the bass will begin to expect the regularly scheduled manna from heaven.

When you detect that, throw more live minnows, then toss a dead one as a ringer. The momentum of their feeding frenzy will compel one of the bass to hit the dead minnow. The next day, throw the live minnows plus two dead ones.

*Increase* the number of dead minnows by one each day; *decrease* the number of live minnows by one each day. Obviously, you'll ultimately throw only dead minnows to the bass, who've grown accustomed to eating them.

Next, throw a dead minnow with a concealed hook and the trained bass will hit it. Let him run with the dead minnow for a few seconds, as he'll swallow it while swimming. With your wrist, snap your pole upright. The hidden hook will tear itself from the minnow and lodge in the bass.

You've got him.

You need not worry about catching all the bass where you found them. As their population dwindles, other bass will take their place. Certain spots in a lake, pond, or river will always have bass unless there is a significant rise or fall in the water level.

In a few days, repeat the process of mixing dead minnows with live. You'll train a new class of bass, as those that preceded them will have graduated to your stringer.

Minnows don't have a long life span. They'll die in hot weather, no matter what precautions you take to keep them alive, including confining them to a container near the surface of the water or a minnow bucket. Using dead minnows instead of buying live ones as replacements is the most frugal way to freshwater fish.

I decided to include this passage because it may be the most topical in these pages. This chapter was written in August 2001, when Cable News Network reported that 400,000 Americans filed for bankruptcy protection against creditors in July. More people sought bankruptcy that month than during any other in United States history.

Bankruptcies and layoffs were predicted to continue. If

so, more and more people will be looking for economical pastimes. Those in stricken income brackets might not want to shell out a few dollars for live bait every time they go fishing. An increasing number will begin fishing to offset the cost of groceries. Fishing with dead minnows will become an economical way to garner nutritional fish, brain food that will enable them to think more like a smart human and determine how in the world they're going to get out of their financial dilemma.

Let the lesson for inactive bait and active bass continue.

After you train bass to eat minnows that have gone to that great shore in the sky, use the same approach to train them to eat virtually anything else they can swallow. Really.

Go back to your fishing spot and toss the dead minnow chum. Occasionally, slip in a piece of domestic meat. Table scraps.

I once taught bass to hit chicken gizzards by systematically tossing them among dead minnows that followed live. I wanted to see if I could get a bass to hit poultry, normally a food that's eaten only by fish that are mostly bottom feeders.

By using the technique outlined above, I eventually put a hook inside a piece of a gizzard, one of the most inexpensive meats in any market. I clobbered the bass because I had earlier trained them to eat gizzards without a hook. Gizzard is tough and resilient. You can catch numerous fish on one morsel.

You can also train a bass to hit virtually anything that will go inside its mouth. My viewers challenged that statement, so I determined that I'd show them how to train bass to strike bait that has always been plentiful and free of charge: tree bark.

I fed the bass live minnows, injected dead ones, then mixed in a tiny and floating piece of tree bark. Wham! A bass hit it so forcefully, the bark came out of the water and fell to the surface. He hit it a second time and took it underwater. It never floated again. He ate something he thought he had killed but hadn't. It was already dead.

I went back to the hot spot the next day and dropped two pieces of bark among the dead minnows. When the bass became accustomed to eating bark, I hid a hook inside a tiny chunk and reeled it through the water, jerking my wrist to make it appear to be alive.

I caught a stringer full of bass on bark. The dry and ragged wood is even tougher, by far, than gizzards. I caught several bass on one sliver of bark. In other words, I caught several pounds of food on bait that will always be free of charge.

I did the same thing after using the same training technique with marshmallows. A marshmallow also floats in the water and becomes a fine top-water lure for bass that are trained to hit them. You can train bass to hit marshmallows more easily than any other food I've found because a soft marshmallow feels good to a bass and because sugar is an underrated bait.

Some might suggest that marshmallows are an expensive food. Not in the long run. If you want to catch bigger fish, put a rabbit pellet inside the marshmallow. It's virtually all protein. A bass trained to hit marshmallows will unknowingly swallow its hidden pellet, and his growth will be markedly accelerated. I've actually "raised" fish to a desired size by training them to hit marshmallows with hidden growth stimulants.

Big fish are more fun to catch, and they provide more food to the table.

Don't forget that bass are like children, as I mentioned earlier. When one has something, the others want it. Train one bass to hit dead minnows, inexpensive chicken gizzards, or tree bark and others will selfishly want it.

Then, after you've caught all the bass you want on these makeshift lures, return to fishing with a Tom Mann creation. Then I'll also have fun and more money to put food on my table.

I made an issue during the '90s of being able to train wild bass, obviously. The more letters of challenge I received, the more lofty were the goals I set for myself. And the more my television ratings climbed.

Letters and e-mails to me ranged from absurd to outrageous. Many were obviously written in jest.

One guy said that if I had any real talent as a fisherman, I'd train a bass to drive a boat. I responded that my skills didn't include training bass to drive a boat, but simply to leap from the water into one. I meant that.

I pointed out that many bass, when caught from a boat, get away as the fisherman tries to heft the bass from the water. If he uses a dip net, the bass or the lure can become entangled in the weave, and the fish will flee. If he tries to raise the bass by hand, he must pinch the bass's bottom lip with his thumb and forefinger. That's a slippery but necessary hold.

If he picks a bass from the water any other way, his fingers will remove the vital coating on the fish's skin. If he puts too many fingerprints on that coating, the fish will die after it reenters the water.

Why not avoid the risk of losing, or killing, a bass by avoiding lifting it into the boat altogether? I told TV viewers that I'd set about the task of training bass that were on my line to leap from the water, through the air, and into the live well in my boat. A live well, you'll recall, is the tank in which caught bass are kept alive.

My promising incredible feats helped me keep a regular, and sometimes skeptical, viewing audience.

And so I regularly trained bass on my line to become bass of the air. I did that many times and never explained how—until now. I developed the following technique by thinking like a fish—how else?

Fishermen usually keep a tight line on a hooked bass. That's wise if the bass is swimming away from the fisherman. If you get slack in your line, the outgoing bass will likely break it. So you must keep your line taut. Yet the more firmly the line is held, the more the hook hurts the bass.

I decided to put my pole forward, thereby taking the pressure off the line, whenever a hooked bass turned to swim toward my boat, not away from it. I reapplied the pressure whenever the bass whirled and darted for open water. The bass soon learned that he could lessen, or eliminate, the pain of the hook by swimming toward the boat.

As he swam toward me, I reeled in line, but never enough to make it tight.

Each time the bass came toward the boat, he came at a greater speed, as he wanted to escape the pain that he didn't know was eased by slack in my line. He only knew that he didn't hurt when swimming in a certain direction.

By the time he made his third or fourth dart toward my boat, he was speeding through the water. I lifted the lid on my live well. I was reeling as he approached the boat and made the line tight when he was two or three feet from it.

There wasn't time for him to turn around, and he didn't want to go under the boat, as he'd also learned that going deeper hurt as much as swimming away. So with his momentum up, his pain level down, and the space between him and the boat depleted, the fish had nowhere to go but upward. He leapt into the air. His inertia, and a midair tug on my line, carried him right into the live well.

I had trained the newly hooked bass, while still on my line, to eliminate pain by soaring into my boat. I've repeated that stunt thousands of times on TV. Some viewers have insisted it's a camera trick.

Such acrobatics are a fun, sure way to avoid losing bass as you try to lift them from the water. It's a trick I try to incorporate at least once into each show I shoot.

As a television host, I've studied successful broadcasters the way I once studied the habits of fish. I noticed that disc jockeys who enjoyed long careers did not necessarily play the hit songs of the day; they played listener requests.

I therefore asked my viewers to tell me what they'd like to see on my programs.

The popularity of bass fishing was at its all-time high in 2001. A consortium of outdoor sporting and recreation companies placed a bounty of eleven million dollars on the head of a bass that weighed more than the world's sixty-year-old record catch.

Many viewers consistently asked that I try to shatter the half-century-old record.

In studying successful broadcasters, I'd learned long ago that they intentionally make their audience feel as if they're part of the program. So I told viewers about the recurring request and asked if any had ever seen a bass that he or she actually thought weighed more than the world record catch.

In time, I received hundreds of responses. The majority pertained to one fish in one lake. Some viewers lived in other states and had gone to the host state strictly to pursue a single bass that was so big, his length had become lore.

That many viewers couldn't be wrong. A freshwater monster whose tail churned him through water had prize money on his head.

I went after him.

I did what I always do when approaching a new lake: I read the water. I saw structure and knew that a bass of the prize bass's suspected size hadn't grown that large through stupidity. He wouldn't be content to hide in generous structure. He'd want an underwater jungle. This bass would be a shrewd swimmer in the watery world of fish, a predator as sly as a guerrilla warrior.

I spotted lily pads. They were dense, like an emerald carpet on the water. If he were in this lake, he'd be hiding somewhere in those pads, I was certain.

Using a trick I mentioned earlier, I drove my outboard through the lily pads, letting its propeller slice the growth to floating fiber. The destruction of structure would flush the bait fish as well as the game fish. The bait fish would scurry back to their hideout, and the sought-after predatory fish would follow. As they did, I'd keep an eye out for the purportedly behemoth bass. A fish that large, when his habitat is disrupted, will often surface.

Even after I turned off the boat engine, the air was filled with a similar noise. It was as if a power lawn mower was at work in the sliced lily pads. I turned around and saw the leaves literally flying through the air.

The big bass plowed through the weed bed with the power of a locomotive. I heard him, and I continued to see the soaring growth shoot out from his self-made path. My churning up the weed bed had left no tunnels out of the thicket.

This super bass was making his own.

I was sure Moby-Dick had a grandchild who had adapted himself to freshwater.

The bass went down and then into open water. How do I know? He was so strong, I could see a swirl rise to the surface wherever he swam. I eased the drag on my line and he ran with it. I was using a thirty-pound test line, which is large enough for a skilled fisherman to land a forty-pound fish easily.

Having seen the bass, I was certain his weight wasn't close to forty pounds, obviously. But I was sure he weighed more than twenty, the fulfillment of my fishing fantasy. This fish, I thought, could be the first one in sixty years to weigh more than the largest largemouth ever caught.

At last my line ran out. The reel could do no more to ease the tension of his powerful pull. I held my pole as high as I could, and it bent as much as its design allowed. There was nothing left I could do to lessen the mighty fish's pull.

And then the boat began to move.

Like something from a tall tale told me by Uncle Alvin and his bootlegging buddy, I experienced a freshwater fish pulling a twenty-one-foot fiberglass boat. That marked the one and only time in my life when I rode in a boat pulled through freshwater by a fish.

I could hear the soft lapping of little waves against the bow of the boat. All I could do was hold on. I didn't do that for long.

My line broke, and my rod recoiled backward far enough to slap me on top of my head. Then silence enveloped me.

No other stillness is quite as unsettling as the calm after the mighty storm brewed by a mighty fighting fish. The snapping of the line is the irreconcilable point of no return for a rod-and-reel enthusiast. When the line breaks, so does his spirit. He thinks about all the things he should have done. But there is nothing he can do after the line is severed.

I involuntarily replayed the entire scene over in my mind—from the time I heard and first hooked the fish, to the short ride across the water in a boat that was practically on his back, to the zing of stretched and snapped monofilament.

I sat motionless in my boat, entertaining a mixture of disbelief and disappointment, all measured by emptiness.

Then he broke water. It was like watching an active volcano, as the great largemouth leapt from the lake and shot skyward. I wondered how far he could hurl himself. I felt my head tilt backward as my eyes followed the fish into the air. As he fell downward, he spun to reveal his other side. There, still in his mouth, was my lure.

I was sure he was goading me, showing me that he'd been as smart as he was large and that his brilliance was responsible for his size. The bass had beaten me and was throwing his victory and my failure in my face. I was sure of it.

I was especially sure when he repeated the gesture and

once again shot toward heaven, my lure still stuck in his mouth. Then he dropped into the water with a giant splash that threw spray all over me.

He had intentionally jumped so close to me that had I not been spellbound, I could have reached out and caught him in the air.

You've no doubt noticed that I haven't mentioned the lake, or the state in which it's located, where I had what may be the largest bass in history on my line. There's a reason for my secrecy.

I'm going back to that lake, and hopefully, to that fish. I think about him frequently, and will for the rest of my life, whether I do or don't catch him.

He's every fisherman's dream of a lifetime. My lifetime won't be complete until my dream becomes my catch.

# CHAPTER NINETEEN

I WAS FISHING my private lake at the end of another busy day in 1999. It was almost nine P.M. My stores were closing for the night and I stood in the dark, watching their lights go off one by one.

I noticed the silhouette of an approaching woman carrying a rod and reel past a sign that read NO FISHING.

What gives with this tourist? I thought.

As she got closer, the woman said she feared she wasn't supposed to be on the private lake, but she had seen me fishing. If I could get away with it, she said, she could too.

"Are there any fish in here?" she asked, looking over the stocked lake.

"I think there's fish," I said, still bewildered.

About that time, I hooked a bass that would weigh two or three pounds. Fishing purely for fun, I was using an ultralight rod, so the tug of the fish seemed like that of a rottweiler. I wanted to play the fish, to take my time as he struggled against the line. I was in no hurry to land him.

The stranger began to explain how to land a fish correctly. I was kidding when I suggested she use my rod to show me just how it's done. She was serious when she took it from my hand.

I watched a trespasser land *my* fish out of *my* lake. She suggested that I pay attention to what she was doing. She knew how to fish correctly, she said, as she had learned a lot from watching Tom Mann on television. She said he owned "those stores," the ones in whose shadows we would have been standing had it not been for darkness.

"Tom Mann lives around here, you know?" she said.

I was unaccustomed to being unrecognized while standing on my own property not two hundred yards from my house.

This, I thought, had to be a joke. It wasn't.

The woman handled her rig—rather, my rig—better than any female I'd ever seen. She had polish and technique. Of course, I could have landed the fish just as skillfully; but then, I didn't have a rod anymore.

She pulled the bass from the water just as a car pulled into the store parking lot, shining headlights on her fish and my face.

"You're Tom Mann!" she said.

Great, both of us know me, I thought, but only one of us knows you.

I asked the woman her name. I'm not easily impressed by amateur fishermen. I knew she wasn't a professional, or I would have known her. I also knew she was good enough to grace any pro's boat.

Such was my introduction to Tina Booker, the first female cohost of a national freshwater fishing show—mine. She joined my program in 2001. By April, the show's ratings had risen by four hundred percent. Today she receives more letters and e-mail than I do. She's admired by both male and female viewers. The men think she's a bombshell; the women think she represents their gender's growing interest in fishing. And both sexes know she's an outstanding fisherman, er, fisherperson. She can do with a spinning rod what Mark McGwire can do with a baseball bat. She's equally as skilled with a fly rod.

Tina can place a lure inside a floating shoebox at twenty yards.

She and her husband were fishing alone once when her bikini top broke, its elastic hurling it into the water. The garment began to float away, and Tina decided to snag it with a lure. She cast her hook and caught the swimsuit top. She's that accurate.

She didn't land her swimsuit, however. As her hook hit the cloth, it was clobbered by a nine-pound bass. For an instant, she had both her fish and her swim top on the line.

As one who gets very excited when she hooks a big fish, Tina began to yell. Boaters and fishermen were attracted to the yelling fisherwoman, the turmoil of the fighting fish, and to other things. Tina was so determined to land the swimming trophy that she disregarded her bikini top. She got her fish, and onlookers got an eyeful. She later recounted the story during a radio contest about true but outrageous events. She won the contest, a small victory to her when compared with taking a nine-pound largemouth.

I got the idea for adding a woman cohost after noticing how many television networks used male and female newscasters. Almost all local news shows around the country were doing likewise.

I had seen the success of television's *Regis and Kathy Lee* and *Crook and Chase,* among others.

Why doesn't someone bring a man-and-woman team to fishing? I wondered. Why don't I?

I contacted a talent agency, which arranged for me to audition some beautiful models from New York City. I'm from the Deep South, where I was graduated from the school of hard knocks. The models were from the Northeast, where they graduated from Ivy League universities.

I had worked for my prosperity; they had grown up with theirs. They were nice people, but we didn't mesh. Worse, they didn't know how to fish.

I had begun to think of Tina during my search for a woman cohost. I'd seen her and her husband, Nelson Booker, many times after our initial meeting. I don't invite many anglers to fish my private ponds. But I issued Tina, her husband, and children a standing invitation. I'd never seen a family who fished from daylight until dark without even stopping to eat. They were as obsessed with fishing as I am.

I became friends with Tina and her family before I employed her. I couldn't be happier with both my professional and personal relationships with the Bookers.

I urged Tina to meet with the talent agents who were trying to cast my show. When she met with interviewers, she told them she had no acting experience and she was as country as corn. Sure that she wouldn't get the part, she hurried through the interviews, thinking, Let's get this over with. I'd rather be fishing.

An agent called to tell me Tina was a natural for the job and strongly recommended that I use her. His advice was unnecessary. I'd already decided to give her a shot.

Tina instantly boosted my ratings more than Jimmy Carter and Radcliff combined. I mean that entirely as the compliment it is.

On one show, I hooked a fish that broke my line and, naturally, disappeared under the water.

"Catch that fish!" I said, kidding as I turned to Tina. She cast her lure about twenty-five yards to the spot where the fish had gone down.

"I've got him," she announced.

In seconds, she lifted a fish that carried my lure in his belly. She'd caught the very fish that I'd told her to catch.

When we aired that, some folks thought it was a technical trick. It wasn't a trick, just incredible fishing. Ask Randy Darrign, my cameraman, or Tom Carter, who helped me write this book. They personally witnessed the feat.

Tina can flat-out fish.

She grew up around Pensacola, Florida, as one of seven children. She was married at fourteen, a mother at fifteen. She had never been outside her native state.

Ten years after her daughter was born, Tina decided to return to school to pursue her general education diploma. She went to school alongside eighteen-year-old boys who called her Blondie or Mom. She took the teasing in stride and graduated with honors.

That done, Tina set her sights on a career in law enforcement, where she would ultimately work as an undercover agent enforcing drug laws in the nation's most cocaine-saturated state.

During training, she underwent eight months of instruction that included grueling physical workouts. She weighed about one hundred pounds, and her partner was a former linebacker. During classes in self-defense, he didn't simply toss her around a mat, he threw her off it.

"Get tough, Tina," an instructor yelled at her. She did, she is.

"If you want something badly enough, and if you believe firmly enough you can do it, you can," Tina said of her quest to enter law enforcement.

She worked as a uniformed officer for five months before going undercover. The usual time in uniform is about two years. But the sheriff's department for which she worked desperately needed a plainclothes female vice officer. Tina fit the bill, although there was little plain about her or her clothes. I call her the new century's answer to Elly May Clampett. She reminds me of Dolly Parton and, like Dolly, she has a brain beneath her piled hair, a heart beneath her . . . well, you know.

While working as a cop, she once posed as a prostitute for a street corner sting. Her father, J. D. Watson, is a religious man. While returning from work, he happened upon Tina working her corner and ordered her off the street, yelling, what did she think her mother would think if she could see her now?!

"And where are your clothes?" he wanted to know.

Tina tried to explain what she was doing, to no avail.

Her suggestive attire had yielded nineteen suspects in ninety minutes. Each man was arrested for solicitation. But a successful sting that had taken several officers weeks to plan was halted in seconds by one daddy.

To please her father, Tina the cop walked away from her busy street corner. She remained in undercover work, however, for five years.

Tina's waistline is eighteen inches, and her waist isn't her most striking feature.

Remember Dolly and the heart part.

Tina works at her figure, doing 250 sit-ups each day, along with other exercise.

She's an attractive woman who was used as bait to a Florida man who'd been terrifying women on the beach by exposing himself. Lawmen tried unsuccessfully to catch the offender.

Then someone got the idea to put Tina in a bikini.

She pretended to be sunbathing, when a man walked up to her. The entire uniformed crime squad was behind her, hiding inside a motor home. Tina wore her swimsuit, a smile, and a surveillance microphone. The cops in the motor home heard the suspect's every word, as well as Tina's response.

"Have you got the time?" Tina told me the man asked.

"Yes," she replied.

"Well, I've got something for you," he continued.

She said the suspect sucked in his stomach and let his swimming trunks fall to the sand. He was naked.

"Well," Tina recalled saying, "I've got something for you."

She pulled a .357 Magnum pistol.

Tina told the man he was under arrest. But she didn't

talk to him long. Still nude, he ran headlong into the cold ocean.

The shore was soon lined with other officers, yelling at the man to come out, as he was going to turn blue from the chill.

He asked for a towel and was given Tina's. She remembered recently that she never did get it back.

She was once shot at with a .44 pistol while pretending to make a drug buy. Tina had appeared on a reality TV show the previous night and was recognized by drug users as an undercover cop.

"Nine-nine-nine," street words for "police," rang through the air. The suspect from whom she was trying to buy cocaine fired at her and ran. He was later arrested and convicted on a string of charges. He's still doing time in prison.

"You don't realize how fast you can run until you're under fire," she told me, saying she didn't return fire because it was too dark, and she didn't want to risk hitting a bystander.

Tina remains unaffected by her newfound fishing fame, except that she deeply appreciates it. During one visit to Eufaula, she went to a Wal-Mart to buy a specific piece of tackle. Seventeen men asked for her autograph. She knows. She counted every one.

She told me that she used to watch every fishing program on television, and think that fishing for a living would be her dream job, never thinking her dream would come true.

She's been married for twenty-six years to the same man. Her house is often a headquarters for her six brothers and sisters, their spouses, and their children, along with her parents.

"My front and back doors are never closed," she said. "I come home two or three times a week and find my house full of family. I love that, and I always will. I will never do anything to discourage the support of family."

Tina and family are no strangers to hard work. They butchered their own meat, and Tina has personally participated in the rolling of hogs, which is the boiling of their carcasses to remove the hair. It's a smelly and sweltering job.

A farm girl who never rose above the roots of her raising, she has cleaned deer and helped cows give birth.

In the spring of 2001, Tina and I were invited to be guests at a bass tournament. Former President George Bush was on hand, and I was eager to meet him. He spent most of his time talking to Tina, however, and sent her an autographed picture of himself, at her request. It hangs in one of my stores today.

Tina and I have a natural chemistry that comes through the camera because we share the same ideas about fishing, agreeing that it's supposed to relieve stress, not cause it. Neither she nor I get mad if a big one gets off the line. She, like me, is not camera shy, and she fishes as if the camera isn't there, recording her every move.

When I first saw how comfortable she was in front of a lens, I was sure she had a background in theater or television. Not so. She's a natural actor because she acts naturally. I like that.

And Tina and I have something else in common. She loves life because, on two occasions, she has almost lost it.

On Easter Sunday night 1997, Tina had left her family

and was en route to join other officers who were scheduled to make undercover drug buys. She drove a little Toyota that was run off the road and into a concrete piling at seventy miles per hour after the car flipped end over end three times. It happened so fast, she never touched her brakes.

Tina's scalp was laid open, and more than half her teeth were scattered around her vehicle. Her collarbone, broken in two, jutted through her skin. Her elbow, forearm, and all the ribs on one side were broken, along with her back in two places, as well as one kneecap.

To this day, she won't go near a small car.

Incredibly, Tina pulled herself from the wreckage. Not one passing motorist stopped to help.

Her mother, at the very instant of the crash, sat up in bed. A religious woman, her mom later indicated that God had told her something was wrong. She began to pray, not knowing for what.

Unable to get help, Tina feared she would bleed to death beside the highway. She turned to look at the earth over which she'd crawled, and spotted her police radio stuck in the ground.

She doesn't say it was miraculously placed there to save her life. She also doesn't say it wasn't.

"I will tell you this," Tina said. "I'm not in church every Sunday ... but my mama is. And my mama was awakened from a dead sleep when the accident happened. My mama was so troubled that she was sitting up in a chair, praying about whatever was wrong, whatever it was. About that time, I figure, is when I found the radio. I have the tape recording of when I called in and said, 'I need help.' "

An all-points bulletin, "officer down," went over the radio.

Earlier, Tina had feared she would bleed to death inside the wrecked car because she could not free herself from the snug seat belt and shoulder strap. Somehow, she got the stubborn snap unbuckled. Or did she?

An investigating officer determined that the belt and strap were firmly snapped in place when he went through the twisted steel. So how did she get out from under the restraints? No one has an explanation as to how she squirmed out of a tight harness and through hopelessly twisted steel.

Four years later, the word "angel" was mentioned in connection with her escape and rescue. Tina again did not say she believed in supernatural involvement. But neither did she say she didn't.

Her mother came to the hospital to pray over Tina.

The bleeding from her head had been so profuse that it was stopped only by direct pressure when another officer put his forehead against hers.

The damage to Tina's body was so extensive, there was hardly any part of her upper body that was not wrapped in a cast. Forty-seven staples were put into her skull to bond her scalp.

And she left the hospital without ever spending a night.

"Another incredible miracle?" Tina was asked.

"My mama had prayed," she said.

Tina's victory over death was not her first. Her most dramatic came three days after her twelfth birthday.

She had been mowing grass, when the lawn mower ran out of gasoline.

"If it runs out of gas, don't ever fill it when it's hot," her dad had told her.

But Tina wanted her dad to be proud of her, and decided to put gasoline into the hot engine so she might finish the lawn.

As she poured the flammable liquid, she dropped the container, and gasoline splashed into her eyes. She immediately knew she should wash the fuel from her face.

By the time she reached the house, the gasoline had run down her body. What she didn't know was that gasoline fumes are more explosive than the liquid itself.

Tina and her mother stood over the kitchen sink, washing Tina's eyes and not thinking about the pilot light on the range beside her. It ignited the fumes from Tina's body, and she was blown into the next room by the blast that engulfed her.

Tina was solid flames from the waist up.

Her brother instinctively grabbed a towel and wrapped it around her. He smothered the blaze in time to save her life, but not before she suffered massive burns.

All her hair was gone, and her head almost instantly swelled to three times its normal size. She was so frightening-looking, she remembers, her own family members began to back away.

That tragedy occurred before her mother knew Jesus Christ personally, Tina said. Her father, she added, had been an alcoholic. Tina said her parents promised God that they would change their ways, and they'd attend church regularly, if He would spare their daughter's life.

He did, and so did they. To this day, her father has never

had another drink. Both parents attend church regularly, and they pray often.

I wasn't surprised to learn that Tina had spiritual beliefs, just as I do, although mine aren't necessarily religious. Her belief in a higher power, whatever she calls that power, is another reason we jelled and became such natural fishing partners and television hosts.

As I said, Tina Booker, after only three months on my show, was largely responsible for quadrupling its ratings. Today, I'm asked about her regularly wherever I go. And as long as I go fishing on television, I don't intend to go without her.

# CHAPTER TWENTY

THROUGHOUT THESE PAGES I have repeatedly stressed that I love what I do. But I sometimes need to get away from the business of fishing for the recreation of it. I suppose that's a lot like a baker making cookies on his day off.

I went fishing for two days simply for the love of it with Ann on September 16, 2001, my sixty-ninth birthday.

My bride of more than a half century and I spent the weekend at Lake Martin, an Alabama lake with cabins often used by newlyweds. Young lovers couldn't have felt any closer than I felt to Ann on my personal holiday.

The cabins are log structures that look as if they were built at the turn of the century, except for running water.

Despite their makeshift amenities, they were nicer than the first home Ann and I shared after our marriage. During those days, we lived in an old-fashioned home because we had to. On my birthday, we lived in old-fashioned surroundings because we wanted to.

I couldn't help thinking that we'd come a long way because we could voluntarily digress to the kind of atmosphere we'd once struggled to escape.

A few days earlier, I had invented a new lure. I wanted to try it out in the clear water of Lake Martin, where, on a sunny day, a fisherman can see twenty feet beneath the surface. I remembered the muddy stream that crossed my daddy's cotton farm, where fishing was largely guesswork, as it was impossible to see beneath the murky surface.

As I watched my new lure go through its paces, and as I modified its infrastructure, I recalled my very first fish hook—a safety pin—given to me by my mother, who was afraid I'd puncture myself with a real hook.

Sweet memories come at unexpected times.

Ann and I spent the entire weekend taking a respite from the pressures of our present day life and the recess prompted a wave of sentimental recollections.

Ann and I had a ball experimenting with my new lure, and sometimes when I hooked a big fish, I handed the pole to her just so she could know the thrill of landing the whopper. I remembered how I had done that the first time I took her fishing. She wouldn't hold her pole when it was baited, as she could not stand the mess of a live worm or minnow that bled on her hands. In those days, I put the bait on the hook, got the fish on the line, and let her pull it to the bank, the most fun part of fishing.

I did that when we were dating because I was eager to show her a good time. I was just as eager on that Indian summer afternoon in 2001.

I had at least fifty of my new lures with me on my birthday outing. Ann and I remembered when we cut corners to buy the raw material to make my very first lure. We not only hoped it caught a fish, we also hoped he didn't strike it hard enough to deform the soft and cheap lead from which it was made. We would have been pressed to scrape together the money to make a replica.

Because of decades in public life, I'm recognized wherever I go. The Lake Martin outing was no exception. Fishermen are not shy, and are forever asking me questions about my life and my fishing techniques.

They often ask what it was like to win those national championships. They want to know what it's like to be on television after eighteen years, a veritable millennium in an industry where programming changes are the rule rather than the exception. People are fascinated because I've been doing new shows every week during a longer first run than was enjoyed by *M*A*S*H*, *Seinfeld*, and even the old classics, such as *The Jackie Gleason Show* and *I Love Lucy*.

I don't think about the longevity of my popularity. I much prefer to think like a fish, and how to improve on that thinking.

I admit, however, that the most pronounced part of my career and popularity has come from television. The success of my television shows lies in their simplicity, and always will.

I remembered one season on ESPN when my show was

so popular that executives wanted to modernize it. I've never understood why some folks have a compulsion to change something that works.

I have intentionally produced almost all of my shows with only one camera. Think about that. Even local news shows use at least two cameras.

With one camera, the viewers can see the entire boat and where my guest fisherman and I are sitting. The big shots at ESPN put two production boats beside my fishing boat. The cameramen were forever getting in the way of my casts. They would shoot a close-up of me, another of my guest, and still another of a fish on the line.

The poor viewers couldn't tell who was catching what. As I watched the replays, I couldn't tell myself. Those days are gone, and today I have the only fishing show on television where my cohost, cameraman, and I sit in the same boat.

I remembered a network with an official who told me that I should begin and end each of my programs with a "how-to" lecture about catching the big ones. I want to entertain folks, not lecture them. Each time I catch a fish, I tell viewers what lure I was using in what depth of water and why I retrieved the way I did. I explain why I'm fishing in whatever spot I have chosen. I make learning fun. People learn a lot more when education is ushered by amusement rather than by formal instructions.

I learned something new on my birthday. I learned that I rarely stop thinking about fishing, but I never concentrate on it. That, perhaps more than anything else, has been the reason for my success as an internationally known angler.

That notion hit me like a bolt from the blue. Fishing is the only sport I know that demands thinking and relaxation at the same time.

That's why I can spend eighteen hours shooting a television show, endure the harsh elements of blinding rain, or rock up and down in a boat until some folks would be seasick. To me, it's all a crazy form of relaxation.

I've known fishermen who are obsessed with catching fish. I've never been obsessed with catching them. I'm just wonderfully taken with the chase which, to me, is more fun than putting the fish in my live well or on a stringer.

My love of the overall fishing process, I realized that weekend, breeds a relaxation that doesn't cloud my thinking or my performance.

I indicated that great memories come when they're least expected. So do profound lessons.

Ann and I departed Lake Martin for the ninety-minute drive back to Fish World and our other enterprises. They're open seven days a week, and it seems that whenever I take two days off, I have to make up the workload of four.

I knew that many fans would be waiting for me, and that some had been inside my store for hours just to get an autograph and photograph with me. Ann still does my bookkeeping, and she'd have to tally the figures that she would have normally calculated at the end of the days we took off.

Those tasks, and many more, would await us as we pulled into the Tom Mann complex after our forty-eight-hour absence.

My calculations indicated that we'd arrive at about

seven-thirty P.M., dusk in September in Alabama. Dusk is a great time to fish.

Before entering one of my stores, I'd sneak off to one of my private ponds. I'd have time to get in at least thirty minutes of fishing before returning to work.

DEDICATION & ACKNOWLEDGMENTS

I dedicate this book to my wife of forty-nine years, Ann, who has been the wind beneath my wings and our family's spiritual leader. Also to my four children: Tommy, Sharon, Cindy, and Nelda.

My son, Tommy, has come a long way in life, and we love him dearly.

Our oldest daughter, Sharon, has worked with us in the businesses since she was six years old. She and her husband, Bill, and their three boys live in Eufaula. She is now my business partner.

Our middle daughter, Cindy, has many talents. She works with arts and crafts and is a brilliant landscaper. She and her husband, Ron, and their son make their home in Eufaula.

Our youngest daughter, Nelda, also has many talents. She is an accomplished artist and sculptor, and teaches art at the local private school. She and her husband, Tracy, and their two daughters make their home in Eufaula.

Finally, in loving memory of my mother, Ethel.

# ABOUT THE AUTHOR

Tom Mann was born in Chambers County, Alabama. A Korean War veteran, Mann is a three-time professional bass fishing world champion, an inductee to the Fishing Hall of Fame, and recipient of the Dophin Award, the highest award bestowed on a professional fisherman. He has sold over one billion fishing lures and is considered one of the world's top lure designers. Mann has been the host of numerous fishing shows on ESPN, TNN, Outdoor, and other networks, and his latest show, *Tom and Tina Outdoors,* airs throughout the South. Mann lives in Eufaula, Alabama.

# ABOUT THE COWRITER

Tom Carter was born in Franklin County, Illinois. He is a former reporter for *Time* and *People* magazines and has written twelve books. Seven of Carter's titles were listed on the *New York Times* bestsellers list during the 1990s.